CW00969721

NEHRU'S INDIA

'An invaluable piece of study and analysis—and an intellectual weapon in the hands of defenders of democracy, secularism and the Constitution'—**Rajmohan Gandhi, research professor, University of Illinois Urbana-Champaign**

'When a colony mutates into an independent nation-state, in a post-colonial situation, the nationalism it supports often changes into a majoritarian identity, and therefore includes only selected citizens. Nehru resisted this. He shunned both majoritarianism and using fascism to advance personal power. Instead, he endorsed the idea of India as a democratic and secular state, as this study demonstrates so decisively'—**Romila Thapar, professor emerita, Jawaharlal Nehru University**

'Pandit Jawaharlal Nehru, the man who led the freedom struggle from [the] front, steered India's transition from colonial rule to a democratic government, envisioned and founded the many institutions necessary for sustaining the newborn democracy and brought a unique combine of socialism and humanism at the centre of India's evolving modernity, has so far remained inadequately understood. Prof. Aditya Mukherjee's depiction of Nehru—the person, the thought and the action—cures that inadequacy with utmost fidelity to historical facts. Anyone desiring to know how India evolved in the decades around Independence and how lasting has been Nehru's contribution to that great transformation must read this work. It is simply outstanding for the depth and the perspicuity with which every essential strand of the unique Nehruvian Consensus has been illuminated'—**Prof. Ganesh Devy, Padma Shri, and winner of the Sahitya Akademi Award**

'Professor Aditya Mukherjee has in this landmark presidential lecture to the Indian History Congress presented Pandit Jawaharlal Nehru as a philosopher–historian–statesman. It is at once courageous, creative and civilizational. Courageous because the neo-fascist forces in India have targeted not only Pandit Nehru as a person but his legacy and the ethos of the Independence Movement itself, with the aim of erasing from history the revolutionary role played by Panditji under the legendary leadership of Mahatma Gandhi. Creative because it required polemical skill as well as research. And civilizational because the Nehru Era, from pre-to post-Independence, formed a new awakening in the Indian subcontinent'—**Kumar Ketkar, senior journalist and former member of Parliament, Rajya Sabha**

'This book must be read widely, just so that the truth be told, as we cherish Nehru's contribution to India's democracy. Why is Nehru a threat to the current political regime and is so demonized? Prof. Aditya Mukherjee expounds Nehru's philosophy and his endeavour to build India as an independent sovereign, democratic, secular and pro-poor nation respecting diversity. He elaborates on how Nehru as a 'man of action' built the institutional framework, structure and culture of politics and economy based on these values. This is so contrary to the imagination of India as a Hindu Rashtra fuelling hatred against the minorities, especially Muslims, requiring fundamental changes in the institutional framework that is fascist and undemocratic. This book is truly inspirational, compelling us to take forward Nehru's imagination of India'—**Prof. Shantha Sinha, Padma Shri, Ramon Magsaysay Award winner and founder–chairperson, National Commission for the Protection of Child Rights**

'Professor Aditya Mukherjee's book comes . . . at a very appropriate moment, marked as it is by a commitment to full accuracy, achieved by profound scholarship. I earnestly hope that it obtains the wide readership it so richly deserves'—**Irfan Habib, professor emeritus, Aligarh Muslim University**

NEHRU'S INDIA

PAST, PRESENT *and* FUTURE

THE **PENGUIN HISTORY** OF MODERN INDIA

ADITYA MUKHERJEE

VINTAGE
An imprint of Penguin Random House

VINTAGE

Vintage is an imprint of the Penguin Random House group of companies
whose addresses can be found at global.penguinrandomhouse.com

Published by Penguin Random House India Pvt. Ltd
4th Floor, Capital Tower 1, MG Road,
Gurugram 122 002, Haryana, India

Penguin
Random House
India

First published in Vintage by Penguin Random House India 2024

Copyright © Aditya Mukherjee 2024

All rights reserved

10 9 8 7 6 5 4 3 2 1

ISBN 9780143471950

Typeset in EB Garamond by MAP Systems, Bengaluru, India
Printed at Thomson Press India Ltd, New Delhi

www.penguin.co.in

For Madhavi . . .
With hope for a better, more humane, future

Contents

Foreword

In inviting me to write the Foreword for his important study of Pandit Jawaharlal Nehru, Professor Aditya Mukherjee has conferred on me an undeserved honour. I have perhaps been his choice partly because the number of persons who can recollect any close encounters with Jawaharlal Nehru, must now, owing to distance in time, be very few indeed. In Jawaharlal-ji's own time, the persons with whom he interacted was, of course, countless; but now more than half a century has passed since his passing away.

Jawaharlal-ji knew my father (Professor Mohammad Habib) because of the latter's close and long association with the Congress. One afternoon in early summer 1942, he suddenly appeared at our house at Aligarh, demanding lunch from my parents, since his hosts, the local Congress organizers, had forgotten all about it! I heard him tell my father, 'We'd be free within five years', despite the gloom that had come upon all of us after the failure of the Cripps Mission.

Twelve years later, in 1954, when I wrote a letter to Pandit Nehru about the denial of a passport to me (for research in England), without making any reference to my father, he immediately gave me an appointment at Delhi (at his office at 9 a.m.). I found all the Central Secretariat offices closed at that time, with no guard or staff member visible around the PM's own office, except his secretary. He gave me twenty minutes— mostly occupied by his own exposition of his perception of the international situation at the time (he was then greatly appreciative of China). He wrote later to my vice-chancellor, Dr Zakir Husain, that he was not fully satisfied with my answers. But despite this, he overruled the Home Ministry's objections, and I received my passport within the next few days.

Later on too, though naturally from a distance, I found the same simplicity and obvious hatred of display on his part. Thrice, he came to Aligarh, when I was a student and later a teacher there, arriving from Delhi invariably in a car with no convoy or other guard car and, while at the University, he freely interacted with teachers and students, again without any security guards.

I also heard him speak more than a couple of times, in both English and Hindustani. In the latter language, he used terms and phrases which reminded one of Ghalib's Urdu. What struck me, when listening to him at Aligarh and London, was not only his modesty but also his deep concern for others—besides, of course, his larger commitment to reason and equity.

Petty jealousies of petty men might now remove his name from institutions and buildings, but so long as truth and reason still find an audience among his people, Jawaharlal Nehru and his work can never be forgotten. It is also incumbent on academics to keep providing to our people the truth about Nehru, his thought and his times. Professor Aditya Mukherjee's book comes, therefore, at a very appropriate moment, marked as it is by a commitment to full accuracy achieved by profound scholarship. I earnestly hope that it would obtain the wide readership it so richly deserves.

Irfan Habib
professor emeritus,
Aligarh Muslim University

July 2024

Preface

This is a revised and considerably enlarged version of my address to the Indian History Congress as its general president in December 2023. At that time, the country was reeling under the ceaseless assault on the secular–democratic 'Idea of India' by 'communal fascist' (a term first used by Amartya Sen) forces. It was this political situation which motivated me to look back at Jawaharlal Nehru, one of the leading proponents of the 'Idea of India', which emerged out of the vision of our freedom struggle, and its chief implementer after Independence, to see what we could learn from him today.

Nehru's non-negotiable, absolute faith in the democratic system, which he refused to 'give up . . . for anything', and his deep understanding of the phenomenon of communalism, which he was the first to see as 'the Indian version of fascism', makes his ideas and practice extremely relevant for us today. I have, in this work, tried to bring out Nehru's complex understanding of communalism and how he combated it; his efforts to transform the Indian economy, ravaged by colonialism, with democracy and sovereignty intact, a unique attempt in global history; his careful building and nurturing of the various institutions on which a democratic system is based; his sophisticated understanding of the discipline of history and his outstanding efforts at writing history; his unrelenting focus on the poor; his promotion of the scientific temper and his anticipation of the knowledge revolution to India's great advantage. In all these areas, India has witnessed a massive regression, particularly in the recent past; much can be learnt from Jawaharlal Nehru in our attempt to resist this downward slide.

In recent years, our youth, women, peasants, independent journalists and sections of the intelligentsia all over the country have demonstrated their capacity to resist this downward slide. During the countrywide agitation against the Citizenship Amendment Act (CAA) in 2019, which clearly targeted the citizenship rights of minorities, the protestors significantly used the democratic Constitution of India as their bible and held aloft portraits of Gandhi, Bhagat Singh, Nehru and Ambedkar! That agitation was brutally quashed on the pretext of the COVID situation and by instigating communal riots. Our farmers and peasants again demonstrated, as they had during our national liberation struggle, their capacity to resist the farm laws brought in by the government in 2020. For months on end, despite untold suffering being inflicted on them, and the efforts to give a communal colour to their protests, they continued protesting till victory was achieved through the repealing of the laws. Numerous civil society initiatives all over the country, like the Constitutional Conduct Group, consisting of a large number of very senior and respected former civil servants, diplomats and former heads of the different wings of the armed forces, continue to strongly critique the government for straying from the democratic path guaranteed by the Constitution. Independent media portals, some newspapers, individual journalists, bodies of intellectuals, writers, actors, stand-up comedians, musicians, historians and human rights activists continue to offer resistance, despite facing severe repression from the state machinery. Opposition parties, with their hands tied behind their backs, their leaders put in jail, their bank accounts frozen and the Enforcement Directorate (ED), Central Bureau of

Investigation (CBI), income-tax departments and other agencies used to intimidate and buy up opposition leaders, nevertheless put up a resistance. A Bharat Jodo Yatra (March to Unite the People of India) and a Bharat Nyay Yatra (March for Securing Social and Economic Justice) led by Congress leader Rahul Gandhi and numerous civil society organizations criss-crossed the length and breadth of the country over several months in 2023 and 2024, holding aloft the Indian Constitution as their mast, raising meaningful issues of the people, despite the heavy odds. It contributed to lifting the pall of fear that was enveloping the country—the fear of the state and the misuse of state institutions, the fear of non-state actors, with the implicit backing of the state, terrorizing people, the fear of poverty, unemployment and so on. In this atmosphere, the call of *'Daro Mat, Darao Mat'* (Do not be afraid and do not create fear in others) by Rahul Gandhi, the current Leader of the Opposition, was a much-needed elixir.

Independent journalists fearlessly took up the challenge of the mainstream media, Controlled by the government and its crony capitalists, which relentlessly promoted government propaganda and was hence nicknamed the Godi Media (literally meaning, media in the lap of the government). These independent journalists used social media to their advantage and, I believe, played a significant part in bringing the truth to the people. This had a bearing on the 2024 elections.

The recent election results of June 2024 have clearly expressed the people's verdict that they wish to arrest the country's rapid slide towards communal fascism. There is a lesson from Nehru even in this partial success in the election. Having destroyed the communal forces in the first general election of 1951–52, despite the highly charged communal atmosphere with large-scale communal killings and millions rendered homeless because of the Partition, Nehru had the following to say: 'One good thing that has emerged from these elections is our straight fight and success against communalism . . . We have seen at last that we need not be afraid of communalism, and we need not compromise with it . . . Where we fight it in a straight and honest way, we win. Where we compromise with it, we lose'. However, he added that the electoral 'success is significant and heartening. But it is by no means a complete success'. An ideological battle along with state power had to be used 'to uproot this despicable communalism. It must be obliterated from the land so that it may not take roots again. This poison . . . has permeated the land.'

When this work was first delivered as a presidential address at the Indian History Congress, the response it received suggested a discontent among the people with the direction in which the country seemed to be headed, a direction opposite to the path envisioned by Nehru. Suggestions were made that it should be translated into various Indian languages to make it more accessible to students and teachers and to enable its use by those engaged in resistance against the formidable challenge to Nehru's 'Idea of India'. I am happy that it is being translated into Hindi and Malayalam, to begin with.

I must, in the end, acknowledge the deep influence on me of the later writings on Nehru by the late Prof. Bipan Chandra, my mentor and then colleague for several decades, with whom I had the privilege of being a co-author. I would also like to thank my family, friends and colleagues who helped make this work possible. Prof. Mridula Mukherjee, my partner in all my ventures, was deeply involved at every step of this work. Others who read the work and made important observations include Profs. Romila Thapar, Irfan Habib, Rajmohan Gandhi, Shantha Sinha, Sven Beckert, Tadd Graham Ferneé, Jane Ohlmeyer, Ganesh Devy, Purushottam Agrawal, Rakesh Batabyal, Mahalakshmi, Gurminder Bhambra, Antoon

De Baets, Manmohan Agarwal, Sebastian Joseph, Gyanesh Kudaisya, Tintu K. Joseph, Salil Misra, Sucheta Mahajan, Alok Bajpai, Comrades Amarjeet Kaur, Shubham Sharma, Kumar Ketkar and Antony Thomas. Finally, I would like to thank Penguin, my publishers, particularly Premanka Goswami, for readily offering to publish this work, making many useful suggestions and then seeing it through in a very short period.

Demonizing of
Nehru

While writing this work for the Indian History Congress, I was deeply aware that the Congress is the largest and most representative organization of historians in India, created during the heyday of the Indian national movement in the mid-1930s. In conformity with the values of our national liberation struggle, symbolized as the 'Idea of India', the Indian History Congress spearheaded the promotion of scientific, secular and anti-imperialist history for over eighty-five years.

This Idea of India is deeply threatened today; the discipline of history is being mauled beyond recognition and weaponized by religious communal forces to destroy the Idea of India.[1] These forces not only did not participate in India's freedom struggle but indeed collaborated with imperialism. It is perhaps appropriate that on his sixtieth death anniversary, I should focus this work on what we can learn from Jawaharlal Nehru, among the foremost champions of the Idea of India, as well as of a scientific and meaningful history. I believe that much can be learnt from him to explain our present and chart out a vision of the future.

It is because of what Nehru stood for that he is demonized so blatantly by communal forces today. All kinds of lies and abuse are spread about him using the massive propaganda machinery that the communal forces command today. Nehru is blamed for all of India's problems, from the Partition of the country, the Pakistan problem, the China problem, the crisis in Indian agriculture, the Kashmir issue, the crisis in the educational system, the persistence of poverty, the growing religious polarization in recent years, amending the Constitution to curb democracy, to almost any problem facing the country today. Truth be told, he is blamed for every pothole in this country. This, nearly sixty years after his passing away! An elaborate website called Dismantling Nehru, with the subtitle 'The last Viceroy of India', is on social media, spreading hatred about Nehru. Hindu communal forces which thought India's Independence was a black day, refusing to unfurl the national flag for many years, today spread falsehoods about one of the country's greatest freedom fighters. A book called *97 Major Blunders of Nehru* has now been expanded to *Nehru Files: Nehru's 127 Historic Blunders*

(*Nehru Ki 127 Aitihasik Galtiyan*). The list keeps growing as new 'facts' are invented. He is even said to have a secret Muslim ancestry, as if having a Muslim ancestry is a crime in itself. Such is the hatred spread about him that one BJP leader, as reported in an RSS journal, went to the extent of saying that Nathuram Godse should have aimed his gun at Nehru.[2] While RSS distanced itself from the write-up published in *Kesari*,[3] it is difficult to imagine that it was not a deliberate effort to demonize Nehru. Apart from spreading lies about him, the effort is also meant to erase his memory from the collective imagination of the Indian people. The iconic Nehru Memorial Museum and Library built on the premises where he lived as the first prime minister of India is no more. Nehru has been dwarfed in that space which now houses a massive museum to all prime ministers (a global first!) and is called the Prime Ministers' Museum and Library. In Rajasthan, it was reported that in the school textbooks created during the BJP regime, 'there is no mention of Nehru either in the chapter (on) Freedom Movement or in India After Independence.'[4] The Indian Council for Historical Research (ICHR), not to be left behind in pushing the BJP government initiative, recently put up a poster, celebrating the seventy-fifth year of Indian Independence, with the pictures of many freedom fighters. However, while Jawaharlal Nehru was excluded from the poster, the name of V.D. Savarkar was added.[5] Replacing Nehru, whose name in the annals of freedom fighters is second only to Gandhiji's with Savarkar, who compromised his nationalist credentials by repeatedly apologizing to the British once jailed, was bad enough. Add to that the fact that after his release, he became the chief ideologue of Hindu communal or supremacist ideology, was the unquestioned leader of the Hindu Mahasabha which cooperated fully with the British during the Second World War at a time when the people of India were sacrificing their lives during the Quit India movement and Jawaharlal Nehru spent nearly three years in jail in Ahmednagar Fort with Maulana Azad, Sardar Patel and other Congress leaders. And then add to it that in the initial murder trial, he was included with the approval of Sardar Patel, the home minister, as a conspirator in Mahatma Gandhi's assassination![6] The ignominy is complete.

Not even the British, who were the chief ally of the communal forces,[7] demonized Nehru in this manner. This despite Nehru spending thirty years of his life fighting the British, with nine of those years spent in

British jails. Though there has been a resurgence of the neocolonial critique of Nehru by people like Tirthankar Roy and Meghnad Desai, among others, it is not crass and vulgar as that done by communalists.

Nehru and the
Discipline of
History

The demonizing of Nehru and the values he represented and stood for could only be done by distorting history and that is what the communal forces have done blatantly. It is, therefore, critically important to begin with a brief discussion on Nehru's own attitude to the discipline of history before moving on to a discussion of how Nehru is being wrongly demonized by detailing some of his actual historic contributions to the making of modern India. I believe that Nehru, since as early as the 1930s, provided a scientific framework, partly demonstrated in his own historical writings, that was in sharp contrast to the colonial and communal framework. Decades later, some of the most distinguished scholars of the country adopted and developed the Nehruvian framework. Much can be learnt from Nehru in this sphere even today.

While referring to Nehru's outstanding historical works, *Glimpses of World History, Autobiography* and *The Discovery of India,* all written in British jails between 1930 and 1944, Professor Irfan Habib made a very significant comparison with Antonio Gramsci's iconic *Prison Notebooks*:

> 'These prison works invite comparison in *both quantity and quality* with the kind of writing that Antonio Gramsci produced as a communist prisoner in fascist Italy. There are true similarities in that both . . . went to history to find answers to the questions raised in their minds as men of action.'[1]

As Nehru himself said, 'Because fate and circumstances placed me in a position to be an actor in the saga, or the drama of India, if you like, in the last twenty or thirty years in common with many others, my interest in history became not an academic interest in things of the past . . . but an intense personal interest. I wanted to understand those events in relation to today and understand today in relation to what had been, and try to peep into the future . . . one has to go back to (history) to understand the present and to try to understand what the future ought to be'.[2] Irfan Habib quoted Marx's famous statement, 'the philosophers have only interpreted the world in various ways, the point is to *change* it', to argue that for a 'man of action' like

Nehru, history was not just a directionless descriptive narrative placed in a chronological order but a resource from which one sought to understand the present in order to try to shape the future.[3]

Nehru urged historians to approach history in this manner. For example, just when India was emerging from the holocaust-like situation caused by communal strife and the Partition of the country on that basis, and the newly born Indian state was to embark on the path of building a secular, inclusive country, Nehru tells historians in December 1948: 'History shows us both the binding process and the disruptive process . . . today a little more obviously—the binding or the constructive forces are at work, as also the disruptive or the fissiparous forces, and in any activity that we are indulging in we have the choice of laying emphasis on the binding and constructive aspect or the other.' While exhorting the historians to emphasize the former, he warns, true to the rigours of the discipline of history, 'We must not, of course, give way to wishful thinking and emphasize something which we want to emphasize . . . which has no relation to fact.' However, he goes on to say, 'Nevertheless, I think it is possible within the terms of scholarship and precision and truth to emphasize the binding and constructive aspect rather than the other, and I hope the activities of historians . . . will be directed to that end.'[4]

This is what Nehru himself did brilliantly in his classic work *The Discovery of India*, while the colonial/communal approach was to constantly try to weaponize any conflict in the past to exacerbate it in the present.

The colonial/communal interpretation repeatedly emphasized the 'trauma' experienced as a result of Hindu–Muslim conflict. These theories of trauma were often created centuries after the so-called traumatic events. A case in point is the alleged trauma felt by 'Hindus' because of the destruction of the Somanatha temple by a 'Muslim' invader, Mahmud, the Sultan of Ghazni (now in Afghanistan) more than a thousand years ago in 1026. After Independence, a demand was made that a grand temple be constructed at Somanatha. K.M. Munshi claimed in 1951, '. . . *for a thousand years Mahmud's destruction of the shrine has been burnt into the collective sub-conscious of the [Hindu] Race as an unforgettable national disaster.*' In fact, there was no evidence of a thousand-year-old trauma. Munshi, perhaps unknowingly, was reflecting the colonial perspective created in the 19th century. Because the earliest mention discovered so far of 'Hindu Trauma' caused by this 'Muslim' invasion in 1026, which had to be avenged, is nearly 800 years later, in 1843 when the issue was brought up in the *British* House of Commons! Colonial historiography since the 19th century has used such events to evolve a notion of permanent confrontation between the Hindus and Muslims, laying the basis of the 'two-nation' theory, which argued that Hindus and Muslims constituted two distinct nations. The communalist picked up this theme and amplified it. The eminent historian Romila Thapar, using a multiplicity of sources, convincingly demonstrated that no such permanent confrontation between Hindus and Muslims occurred historically as a result of the destruction of the Somanatha temple. One hundred and fifty years after its destruction, a Hindu king rebuilt the Somanatha temple without even a mention of Mahmud having destroyed it. Two hundred and fifty years later, land was given to a Muslim trader to build a mosque on land belonging to the estates of the same temple with the approval of the local Hindu ruler, local merchants and priests! No signs of a 'trauma' in the 'collective memory' of Hindus is visible until it was a 'memory' constructed much later under colonial patronage by their allies, the religious communal forces.[5] Destruction of religious places was routinely carried out *across religions and sects* often to loot the wealth of these institutions or to establish authority in ancient and medieval times and was perhaps treated as such. Nehru himself had a much more nuanced account of Mahmud Ghazni than that portrayed by the colonial/ communal combine, where he sees him as 'far more a warrior than man of faith' who used his army raised in India under a Hindu general named Tilak, 'against his own co-religionists in Central Asia'.[6]

The nationalist intelligentsia in the colonial period put forward a totally different interpretation of Indian history from the colonial/communal one, where they were not trying to create memories of historical 'trauma' in order to create differences in the present. On the contrary, they drew on the reality of Indian society and how it organically dealt with religious, caste and other difference through the birth of new religions like Buddhism, Jainism and Sikhism or movements spanning many centuries like the Sufi and Bhakti movements. Jawaharlal Nehru perhaps best argued this position in his magisterial magnum opus, *The Discovery of India,* written from prison in the early 1940s. The lessons that Nehru tried to draw from Indian history were connected to his imagining of *India's future as a modern democratic country based on enlightenment values, 'the Idea of India'*. He focused on some critical aspects of India's civilizational history; an openness to reason and rationality, a questioning mind and an acceptance of multiple claims to truth, a dialogical tradition of being in conversation and discussion with each other, the ability to live with difference, accommodate, adjust, resolve and transform rather than violently crush difference. Further, given the current push towards a narrow, 'frog in the well' outlook, Nehru made a significant observation about Indian history:

'If we look back at India's long history we find that our forefathers made wonderful progress whenever they looked out on the world with clear and fearless eyes and kept the windows of their minds open to give and to receive. And in later periods, when they grew narrow in outlook and shrank from outside influences, India suffered a setback politically and culturally.'[7]

Interestingly, Amartya Sen, makes similar arguments and expands on both these themes in a number of his writings, decades later.[8]

Nehru drew from the Indus valley civilization, the Rig Veda, the Upanishads, the epics Ramayana and Mahabharata, the Gita, Buddha, Asoka, Alauddin Khilji, Amir Khusrau, Akbar, Vivekananda and Gandhiji to illustrate the above. He also emphasized how shared traditions in language, music, poetry, painting, architecture, philosophy and everyday practice, cutting across religion and caste, contributed to the creation of a composite culture. While talking of songs composed by Amir Khusrau he said, 'I do not know if there is any other instance anywhere of songs written 600 years ago (in the ordinary spoken dialect of Hindi) maintaining their popularity and their mass appeal and being still sung without any change of words.'[9] He talked of the emergence of the Indian civilization that occurred over the centuries through the 'absorption', 'assimilation' and 'synthesis' of all the influences India was exposed to through trade, invasions, migration and intermixing. From the Indus Valley civilization 5000 years ago to the Dravidian, Aryan–Central Asian, Iranian, Greek, Parthian, Bactrian, Scythian, Hun, Arab, Turk, early Christian, Jewish, Zoroastrian, Afghan, Mughal, etc., all leaving their mark:

'like some ancient palimpsest on which layer upon layer of thought and reverie had been inscribed, and yet no succeeding layer had completely hidden or erased what had been written previously.'[10]

It is to this organic process through which the Indian people had learnt to negotiate differences of multiple religions, languages, castes, etc., that colonialism came as a shock. It was as if Indian history 'ceased', to use a word used by the African revolutionary Amilcar Cabral for the period of colonial rule lasting nearly 200 years. Colonialism not only stopped the dynamic process of negotiating differences but actually froze or even accentuated these differences. And the communal forces were the chief instruments in their hands for accomplishing this task. The world has learnt at a very heavy cost, from Ireland, the oldest colony, to recent events in Palestine (about the Imperialist role on which Nehru has much to say) and the experience of large parts of Asia and Africa, including India, that the longest lasting legacy of colonialism has been that it left behind a divided people.

One method used by the colonial/communal forces to create a religious divide, of which Nehru was very critical, was the colonial periodization of Indian history, done by James Mill in the early 19th century, 'into three major periods: Ancient or Hindu, Muslim and the British period.' He thought 'it is *unscientific* to divide history like this' and said, 'This division is neither intelligent nor correct; it is deceptive and gives a wrong perspective. It deals more with the superficial changes at the top than with the essential changes in the political, economic and cultural development of the Indian people'.[11] He said, 'It is wrong and misleading to talk of a Muslim invasion of India or of the Muslim period in India, just as it would be wrong to refer to the coming of the British to India as a Christian invasion, or to call the British period in India a Christian period.'[12] He questioned the defining of a period by just the religion of the ruler and emphasized the wider social, economic and cultural factors which defined a period. He also pointed out the continuities and cultural intermixing of people belonging to different religious faiths. Later historians have confirmed Nehru's position while critiquing the colonial/communal periodization of Indian history.[13]

In fact, Nehru was extremely critical of looking at history with 'the old and completely out-of-date approach of a record of doings of kings and battles and the like'. He said: 'The whole conception of the history of a country being the names of a large number of kings and emperors and our learning them by heart, I suppose, is long dead. I am not quite sure whether in the schools and colleges of India it has ceased to exist or not, but I hope at any rate that it is dead, because anything more futile than children's study of the record of kings, regions and battles I cannot imagine.'[14]

On the contrary, Nehru, anticipating what has now globally become an accepted norm in cutting-edge historiography, emphasized 'the social aspect of history'. The need for 'much closer research into the daily lives of the *common man*. Maybe in *family budgets* a hundred or a thousand years ago . . . which make us realize something of what the life of humanity was in the past age.' As he put it in his characteristically beautiful prose, '*It is only then that we really clothe the dry bones of history with life, flesh and blood.*'[15]

Nehru was deeply aware of the various biases in history writing and very critical of the Eurocentric and colonial approaches which often overlapped, and which unfortunately exercise considerable influence in the former colonies till today.[16] Giving his inaugural address to the Asian History Congress, Nehru said: 'The immediate object of the History Congress should be to straighten out all the twists which Asian history has received at the hand of the Europeans. While some of them are very fine historians, their approach has nevertheless been based on Europe being the centre of the world.'[17] He continued, 'In the case of India, a Western scholar, especially from the United Kingdom, inevitably tended to look at the history of India as if the past few thousand years were a kind of a preparation for the coming British dominion in India.' However, Nehru warned that 'as a reaction to that sometimes our own historians have gone too far . . . There is the nationalist history which, starting from a strong nationalist bias, praises everything that is national at the expense of other things.'[18] As early as the 1930s, reacting to the nationalist tendency to imagine a 'Golden age' in the past which the communalists used to create a religious divide, a tendency that has become rampant today, he said: 'Everywhere are to be found people who consider their own country the best, and regard it as sacred soil. They only study their ancient history and award it a high place—it becomes Satyayug or Ramrajya; and the hope remains that the same may be restored.'[19] He argued, 'Both these approaches . . . the nationalist approach and imperialist approach distort history. They sometimes suppress history.'[20] Nehru showed in his own writing in the *Glimpses of World History* and *The Discovery of India* how one could be firmly anti-imperialist and also have pride in one's own history— for the *genuine* achievements without resorting to blind imaginary glorification of one's past overlooking all the warts and blemishes.

While on the subject of Eurocentric/colonial positions, Nehru very early on refutes the tendency to obfuscate the difference between the empires of the ancient and medieval period and the modern colonial empires emerging with the rise of capitalism. A tendency which has continued till today.[21] He says as early as 1933, '. . . There have been vast empires for thousands of years, but modern imperialism is a new concept developed for the first time in recent years . . . But very few of us have understood its real import and often mistake it for imperialism of the old. Unless we understand this new imperialism properly and discern its roots and branches, we cannot grasp the conditions of the present-day world and cannot properly wage our battle for freedom.'[22] In fact, throughout the pages of the voluminous *Glimpses of World History,* Nehru maintains and highlights this clear distinction and explores the very complex evolution of modern imperialism.

Nehru repeatedly questions the colonial characterization, picked up by the communalists, of the medieval period when many of the rulers in India were Muslims, as 'foreign rule', clearly *distinguishing it* from British colonial rule, which he described as foreign rule. Lest one thinks it is stating the obvious, it should be pointed out that our current prime minister repeatedly, from the ramparts of the Red Fort in his Independence Day speech, his speech in Parliament as prime minister in 2014, his address to the US Congress in 2023, etc., has reiterated the RSS position and talked of 1000 years of foreign rule (sometimes he makes it 1200, presumably 200 years is of little relevance in a long history). With one stroke, all Muslim rulers were declared as foreigners from whose alleged loot and 'slavery' India had to win Independence![23] The paradox is that the forces which did not play a part in the *actual* struggle for freedom against British colonial rule, except to weaken the national movement against it, talk of freedom from a so-called 'Muslim' rule in the *medieval* period! Nehru, while critiquing the 'Hindu, Muslim and British period' characterization (discussed above) commented on this aspect, distinguishing the medieval period, when many rulers were Muslim in India, from the British period which is what he saw as a period of foreign rule. He said:

'The so-called (Hindu) ancient period is vast and full of change, of growth and decay, and then growth again. What is called the Muslim or medieval period brought another change, and an important one, and yet it was more or less confined to the top and did not vitally affect the essential continuity of Indian life. The invaders who came to India from the north-west, like so many of their predecessors in more ancient times, became absorbed into India and part of her life. Their dynasties became Indian dynasties and there was a great deal of racial fusion by intermarriage. A deliberate effort was made, apart from a few exceptions, not to interfere with the ways and customs of the people. *They looked to India as their home country and had no other affiliations. India continued to be an independent country.*

The coming of the British made a vital difference and the old system was uprooted in many ways. They brought an entirely different impulse from the west, which had slowly developed in Europe . . . and was taking shape in the beginnings of the industrial revolution. The British remained outsiders, aliens and misfits in India, and made no attempt to be otherwise. Above all, for the first time in India's history, her political control was exercised from outside and her economy was *centred* in a distant place. They made India a typical colony of the modern age, a subject country for the first time in her long history.'[24]

A few more points on Nehru and history writing which are relevant to us even today.

From very early on, Nehru was a votary of looking at history in a global context. He was an exponent of what is now fashionably called 'connected histories.' He said, 'The old idea of writing a history of any one country has become progressively out of date. It is impossible today to think of the history of a country isolated from the rest of the world. The world is getting integrated. We have . . . to consider history today in a world perspective.'[25] Globally, 'events are all closely inter-related. One event affects the other and if all the developments of world history are taken together then some sort of laws and causes emerge and we can understand the course and significance of world history. By knowing this some light is thrown on all events of world history and we can *see our course ahead.*'[26] Further he said, 'It is quite impossible today to think of *current events or of history in the making* in terms of any one nation or country or patch of territory; you have inevitably to think of the world as whole.'[27]

As a 'man of action', one who contributed significantly to the making of history, Nehru saw the need to keep the *big picture* in mind while approaching history. He said, 'It has been given to us in the present age to play a part in the making of history and for a person who does that it becomes an even more important thing to understand the *process of history* so that he might not lose himself in trivial details and forget the main sweep.' He urged the historians too not to get lost in the details, so that they may 'see the wood a little more and not be lost in the individual tree'. He added, 'Any subject that you may investigate' should 'be viewed in relation to a larger whole. Otherwise, it has no real meaning except as some odd incident which might interest you.'[28]

Again, as a man of action, Nehru urged 'historians . . . that they should not always write only for their brother historians . . . for the charmed circle of people who are interested in a specifically narrow aspect' which 'loses all interest for the wider public'. They should 'try to appeal to the minds of the larger public—the intelligent or semi-intelligent public.' He did not believe that 'popularization . . . means a deviation from scholarship. I do not think there is any necessary conflict between real scholarship and a popular approach.'[29] He had as early as 1933 urged that 'books should be written not for a few scholarly persons but should be such that a person with very limited reading—a farmer or a labourer even—should be able to understand it. Unless the masses understand it, our labour would be in vain.'[30] Some of the tallest scholars in India, inspired by the Nehruvian dream, did try to do what he desired, writing texts for young schoolchildren, popular pamphlets and books,[31] while others, often in the name of the poor and the subalterns, went into a postmodernist discourse which at least I, even after more than four decades of trying to understand the discipline of history, have great difficulty even in beginning to decipher.

Finally, a comment on how Nehru saw his role in taking the historical process forward.

The lessons he learnt from Indian history of the acceptance of the existence of multiple truths, of a non-violent dialogical tradition, of negotiations of truth claims and conflict and arriving at a higher level of synthesis, were greatly strengthened by his increasingly deeper understanding of Gandhiji and his practice. This involved a change in his own Marxist understanding which he had argued till the mid-1930s, as seen in the *Autobiography,* towards a more complex Gramscian Marxist understanding of how social change was to be negotiated.[32] His more mature *understanding* was reflected in The *Discovery.* (More on this aspect later.) This shift has often been seen as Nehru's contradictory and vacillating nature, his total dependence and subservience to Gandhiji, his giving in to vested interests, etc.[33]

In an insightful work, Manash Firaq Bhattacharjee sees Nehru's doubts, his ambivalence, openness and engagement with apparently contradictory positions not as his weakness or vacillating nature but as his *strength.* He is correctly critical of people like Partha Chatterjee who dismiss Nehru's absolutely outstanding work, *The Discovery of India,* as a book of 'rambling, bristling with the most obvious contradictions.'[34] (Other scholars such as the Eurocentric Marxist Perry Anderson also shockingly rubbish Nehru's *Discovery* calling it 'a steam bath of *Schwärmereii* (over-enthusiastic and sentimental)' with a 'Barbara Cartland Streak'![35]

As Bhattacharjee argues in elegant prose:

'The idea of liberty needs to be reconciled with the presence of contradictions. No idea or truth–claim can justify the sacrifice of human lives. It would mean the barbarism of truth. Ethics provokes us to think of freedom without violence.

Nehru did not sit on horseback with sword in hand, and rush towards the windmills of history thinking they were giants he had to exterminate. He did not hallucinate from the desire to rid the world of all its ills and create a gigantic prison in the name of paradise'[36]

This is where Nehru learnt from Gandhiji. He accepted Gandhiji's position that however good the end, the means had to be ethical and non-violent.[37] For Gandhiji, his deep conviction in non-violence did not emerge from the fact that it was a brilliant tactic to fight the British, which of course it was, but from his philosophical position that nobody could make the claim of having arrived at 'transcendental truth' or absolute truth. His belief in the possibility of multiple truths and multiple paths to the seeking of truth would not allow for violence against anyone. The Enlightenment project emerging from Europe often faltered on this ground, where the notion of possessing the ultimate truth justified mass killings by revolutionary movements (in the name of democracy and the people), thus negating a critical aspect of democracy: every human being's right to differ. Gandhiji saw this weakness in the French and the Russian Revolution as compared to India's struggle for freedom.[38] Attention must be drawn here to Tadd Graham Fernée's work, where he compares the European Enlightenment project with the Indian, Turkish and Iranian efforts at transition to modernity, with a focus on the Indian National Movement under Gandhiji's leadership with its 'Ethic of Reconciliation as Mass Movement' as well as the 'Nehruvian effort after Independence' at drawing on this heritage, towards an 'Ethic of Reconciliation in Nation-Making'.[39] His conclusion is that the Indian experiment at transition to modernity without violence remained much truer to the Enlightenment objectives.

Bhattacharjee has done us a favour by quoting extensively from Octavio Paz,[40] the great Mexican poet, thinker, diplomat and Nobel Laureate, who was also the Mexican ambassador to India in Nehru's time, showing how he very sensitively comprehended what Nehru had 'discovered' for himself from Indian tradition and Gandhiji and, very importantly, how he brilliantly interpreted Nehru and his supposed contradictions. It is well worth repeating them here, if for no other reason than to show how great contemporaries of Nehru saw him in contrast to scholars whom I would characterize as Eurocentric, if not colonial, and of course, the communal, fake 'nationalists' in India.

In a speech delivered in 1966, Paz says:

'It is remarkable that Nehru, in spite of his mainly being a political leader, did not fall into the temptation of suppressing the contradictions of history by brute force or with a verbal *tour de passé* (sleight of hand). [It] is unique in our world of fanatical Manicheans (those who see things only in black and white) and hangmen masked as philosophers of history. He did not pretend to embody either the supreme good or the absolute

truth but human liberty: man and his contradictions
. . . He was faithful to his contradictions and
for this very reason he neither killed others nor
mutilated himself.'

Again, he says very profoundly and with a deep
understanding of Nehru:

'In contrast to the majority of the political leaders
of this century. Nehru did not believe that he had
the key to history in his hands. Because of this he
did not stain his country nor the world with blood.'

Nehru tried to move towards his goal, what he
thought was his historic role with this sensibility. This
meant following a path which could be slower, but took
people along and did not resort to violence and brute
force as many of his contemporaries, trying the same
transformation, did.

Nehru and the
Idea of India

We may ask ourselves the question that if Jawaharlal Nehru was indeed the blundering, Westernized, alienated-from-Indian-reality persona that he is made out to be by his naysayers, why did the father of the nation, Mahatma Gandhi, choose *him* as his successor and not his other brilliant comrades like C. Rajagopalachari or Sardar Patel?

In a speech at the All India Congress Committee (AICC) meeting at Wardha on 15 June 1942, Gandhiji declared:

'. . . Somebody suggested that Pandit Jawaharlal and I were estranged. This is baseless . . . You cannot divide water by repeatedly striking it with a stick. It is just as difficult to divide us. I have always said that not Rajaji, nor Sardar Vallabhbhai but Jawahar will be my successor . . . When I am gone . . . he will speak my language too . . . Even if this does not happen, I would at least die with this faith.'[1]

Why did Gandhiji have such tremendous faith in Jawaharlal Nehru? One can surmise at least two reasons.

First, Jawaharlal Nehru quintessentially represented and fought for all the core values of the Indian freedom struggle which have in short been called 'The Idea of India'. These core values were in brief:

1. Sovereignty, i.e., India will be independent and self-reliant, and oppose imperialist domination globally.
2. Democracy, i.e., India will be a democratic country with adult franchise and with *equal rights* to all citizens, irrespective of their caste, class, religion, language, gender, region or ethnicity.
3. Secularism, i.e., people belonging to different religious faiths will have equal rights in the country. India will *not* be a majoritarian Hindu state. Secularism and democracy were seen as coterminous, one could not exist without the other. The term secular–democracy was often used conjointly, just as communalism was with loyalism.

4. Pro-poor orientation. Beginning from the early nationalists like Dadabhai Naoroji whose book was titled *Poverty and Un-British Rule in India* to Gandhiji turning the face of the country towards the poor, the *Daridranarayan*, to the revolutionaries, socialists and communists— all were agreed on a pro-poor orientation even if there was no consensus on socialism or communism.

5. Modern scientific outlook was to be propagated (what Nehru called the scientific temper), overcoming obscurantism and blind faith.

It must be noted that there was a consensus among the entire spectrum of the Indian national movement on these core values whatever may have been their other differences. From the early nationalists like Dadabhai Naoroji, M.G. Ranade and Gopal Krishna Gokhale, to Lokmanya Tilak and C.R. Das, to Bhagat Singh and other revolutionaries, to Gandhiji, Nehru, Sardar Patel, Subhas Chandra Bose, socialists like Acharya Narendra Dev and the early Jayaprakash Narayan and communists like E.M.S. Namboodiripad, Harkishan Singh Surjeet and P.C. Joshi, all agreed on the above core values of the Idea of India. Only the loyalists and the communalists of all hues were opposed to them.

Not only did Jawaharlal Nehru fight for these values during the freedom struggle but he also played a stellar role in *implementing* these ideas in the newborn state after Independence. Gandhiji perhaps anticipated this capacity of Nehru in choosing him as his successor. In fact, the burden of implementing these ideas fell largely on Nehru's shoulders with the Mahatma being murdered by a Hindu communalist within six months of India gaining Independence and Sardar Patel passing away in 1950. Nehru performed this task with great élan and imagination as India's first prime minister for about seventeen years.

It is on Nehru's role after Independence in implementing the five core values of the 'Idea of India' that I will focus on today. It is necessary to do so as each element of the Idea of India is deeply threatened today.

When we evaluate Nehru's role in implementing the Idea of India after Independence, we must remind ourselves of what economists call the 'initial conditions' from which he had to start, to get an idea of the gigantic task ahead of him at Independence. The poet

Rabindranath Tagore, shortly before his death, had graphically anticipated the condition of India at the end of British rule. He said:

'The wheels of fate will someday compel the English to give up their Indian empire. What kind of India will they leave behind, what stark misery? When the stream of their centuries' administration runs dry at last, what a waste of mud and filth will they leave behind them . . .'[2]

The 'mud and filth left behind' was a famine-ridden country (three million perished in a man-made famine just four years before Independence), where per capita income and foodgrains output had been actually *shrinking* annually for three decades before Independence, where the *average* life expectancy at Independence was a shocking low of about thirty years, 84 per cent of all Indians and 92 per cent of women were illiterate. On top of all this, the British left the country deeply divided on religious lines, with millions dead and rendered homeless in a religious communal carnage that happened under colonial tutelage.[3]

It was a gigantic task indeed to lift India out of this misery following the path laid down by our freedom fighters in their imagination of independent India. It is to Nehru's credit that he evolved a multipronged strategy to lift India out of this morass, which in fact became an example for numerous other countries that gained Independence from colonial rule.

I will seek to outline how Nehru undertook this stupendous and, in many respects, historically *unique* task of creating a modern democratic nation state in a plural society left deeply divided through the active collusion of the colonial state; of promoting modern industrialization within the parameters of democracy in a backward and colonially structured economy; of finding the balance between growth and equity in an impoverished, famine-ridden country; of empowering the people and yet expecting them to tighten their belt for the sake of the nation as a whole; of promoting the highest level of scientific education, a field left barren by colonialism; in short, of un-structuring colonialism and bringing in rapid economic development but doing it consensually, without the use of force, keeping what has been called the *'Nehruvian consensus'* intact in the critical formative years of the nation. A Herculean effort was needed to achieve this complex task and Jawaharlal Nehru rose to the occasion, putting everything he had into this effort, in the process leaving behind a legacy not only for the Indian people but for all the people of the world oppressed by colonialism, who were striving to liberate themselves of their past, but in a humane and democratic manner.

I may mention here that I have not dealt in this work, except in passing, with Nehru's enormous contribution to the shaping of India's foreign policy and indeed his emergence as a global statesman influencing deeply global politics. Nehru's foreign policy again had deep roots in the vision of our national movement and the Idea of India. It is a complex area which requires a separate, detailed analysis, particularly because much ill-informed abuse is hurled at him for his alleged foreign policy failures by his right-wing communal detractors.

Nehru spearheaded the non-aligned movement, leading a large number of post-colonial countries into staying out of the cold-war politics indulged in by the superpowers after the Second World War. Instead of becoming pawns in the hands of these superpowers, the movement was to encourage member countries to focus on their own independent economic development and their hanging together to prevent colonial domination from re-emerging in the world. (His efforts at Afro–Asian unity were aimed in this direction.) It is not for nothing that over a hundred countries were persuaded to become a part of the non-aligned movement over time. Nehru played a major role in promoting world peace and in protesting against the race for nuclear weaponization. He played a critical role in defusing conflict during the Korean War, the Suez Crisis and the Vietnam War, preventing the break-up of and recolonization of Congo, liberating Goa, and promoting the Panchsheel, the principles of peaceful coexistence among countries, which acquired much salience in international relations globally. It is not surprising that future prime ministers of India, including his bitter critics like Atal Bihari Vajpayee remained within the broad parameters laid down by Nehru in the area of foreign policy. As his one-time brutal critic, Winston Churchill was to concede in a letter to Nehru:

'I always admired your ardent wish for peace and the absence of bitterness in your consideration of the antagonisms that had in the past divided us. Yours is indeed a heavy burden and responsibility, shaping the destiny of your many millions of countrymen, and playing your *outstanding part in world affairs.* I wish you well in your task. Remember 'The Light of Asia'.'[4]

Nehru on the Communal Challenge

The secular vision of the Idea of India was severely threatened at the point of the very birth of the independent Indian nation state, as it is threatened today. Much can be learnt from how this threat was dealt with by our nationalist leaders. The communal challenge, in my opinion, being the most important challenge before our country today, I shall discuss this aspect in somewhat greater detail than the other aspects of the Idea of India that are also endangered.

The period 1946–52, from the time Jawaharlal Nehru took over as the head of the Interim government till he, as prime minister, led independent India into its first general election, was the phase when the secular 'Idea of India' was tested against the most overwhelming odds. Independence was accompanied by the Partition of the country and widespread religious communal violence. It was a holocaust-like situation where an estimated 5,00,000 were killed and millions were rendered homeless (nearly six million refugees poured into India) in a spate of communal hatred and violence.

The result was one of the largest transfers of populations in human history in a short span of just a few years. In the midst of all this, the tallest leader of the fledgling Indian nation, Mahatma Gandhi, the Father of the nation, was felled by an assassin's bullet, an assassin who was put up to challenge the very 'Idea of India' the Mahatma had lived and died for. In this atmosphere of hatred and violence, guiding India to its first democratic general election based on complete adult franchise appeared to be a nearly impossible task. But Jawaharlal Nehru took the challenge head on and with indomitable energy saw India through its worst ever crisis at the very moment of its birth as a new nation. It was, in the words of an Indian historian in a recent study, his 'finest hour'.[1]

A spiral of religious sectarian violence engulfed India in the run-up to Independence and Partition. It began with the Great Calcutta Killings as a result of the Muslim League's call for Direct Action in August 1946, barely a month before the Interim government, led by Nehru, was set up in September by the British as a prelude to the handing over of power. The very next month, in October, large-scale violence erupted in Noakhali, a remote district of Bengal, with the Muslim League government that ruled the province doing little to stop it. As a reaction to the violence against Hindus in Calcutta and Noakhali, large-scale violence against Muslims broke out in neighbouring Bihar, spreading like wildfire, for the first time in rural areas.

Gandhiji immediately rushed to the villages of Noakhali on 6 November 1946 to take on the most difficult task of trying to contain communal violence with a hostile Muslim League government in power in the province. At a time when perhaps one of the most important events of world history, the preparation for transfer of power from the British Empire to a free India, a transfer which was followed by colonial empires collapsing in most parts of the world, was taking place, the top leader of the Indian national movement which ousted the British, *spent four months*, till 4 March 1947, walking on village paths and sleeping in huts in hamlets in this virtually unreachable, remote corner of India. This was at a time when the complex negotiations for the transfer of power were under way! This showed the utmost importance Gandhiji placed on fighting communalism. Nehru, on his part, rushed to Bihar, and between 4 and 9 November 1946, along with virtually the entire top leadership of the Congress—Sardar Patel, Rajendra Prasad, Maulana Azad, Acharya Kripalani,

Jayaprakash Narayan, Anugraha Narain Sinha—and many others toured the affected areas, determined to stop the violence immediately. 'One by one, he (Nehru) brandished all the weapons in his armoury, the coercive power of the state, the prestige and ideals of the freedom struggle, the prestige and reverence for Gandhiji, his own personal prestige, and much else'[2] to bring things under control. He put his own life at stake and declared immediately on reaching Bihar:

'I will stand in the way of Hindu–Muslim riots. Members of both the communities will have to tread over my dead body before they can strike at each other.'[3]

By 8 November, things were under control in Bihar.

Independence came with hundreds of thousands of refugees pouring into East Punjab and Delhi, and large-scale violence ensued in this region. In his Independence Day speech from the ramparts of the Red Fort in Delhi on 16 August 1947, Nehru made it clear that communal strife would not be tolerated and that India would be a secular state, and not the mirror image of Pakistan, a Hindu state. He declared:

'The first charge of the Government will be to
establish and maintain peace and tranquillity in the
land and to ruthlessly suppress communal strife . . .
It is wrong to suggest that in this country there
would be the rule of a particular religion or sect. All
who owe allegiance to the flag will enjoy equal rights
of citizenship, irrespective of caste and creed.'[4]

The very next day he was in Punjab and in the first
few weeks after Independence he was more in Punjab
than in Delhi. Again, in a broadcast to the nation on 19
August 1947, he asserted in no uncertain terms:

'Our state is not a communal state but a democratic
state in which every citizen has equal rights. The
Government is determined to protect these rights.'[5]

Barely had the communal situation come under
control when Mahatma Gandhi was assassinated. About
the immediate action taken, Nehru said, 'We have
banned the Rashtriya Swayam Sewak Sangh . . . enough
has come to light already to show that this assassination
was not the act of just an individual . . . behind him
lay a fairly widespread organization and deliberate

propaganda of hate and violence . . . '[6] In fact he saw it as an effort to change the very nature of the Indian state by seizing power. In his letter to the chief ministers on 5 February 1948, he did not mince his words:

> 'It would appear that a deliberate *coup d'etat* was planned involving the *killing of several persons* and the promotion of general disorder to enable the particular group concerned *to seize power*. The conspiracy appears to have been a fairly widespread one, spreading to some of the states.'[7]

It was a threat to the very 'Idea of India' as a secular country and Nehru was not about to let it succeed. With the full support of his Home Minister and Deputy Prime Minister Sardar Patel, he not only banned the RSS but also jailed 25,000 of its activists. Even when the ban on the RSS was removed in July 1949, after it gave written assurances that henceforth it would function only as a cultural organization and have nothing to do with politics, he warned the chief ministers of the fascist nature of the RSS and the threat of their renewing their activities.[8]

Nehru's commitment to the secular ideal and his prescient understanding of the grave nature of the threat from the communal forces is evident from the manner in which he converted the first general elections of 1951–52 into a virtual referendum on what was to be the nature of the Indian state. Was it going to be a 'Hindu Rashtra', a mirror image of 'Muslim Pakistan', or a secular–democratic Indian state? He made the fight against the communal political groups his central objective and campaigned relentlessly for realizing the secular vision of the Indian national movement. 'He travelled nearly 40,000 kilometres and addressed an estimated thirty-five million people or one-tenth of India's population. The result was that in a peaceful fair election held within years of the holocaust-like situation and extreme arousal of communal frenzy, the communal parties, the Hindu Mahasabha, the newly formed Jana Sangh, and the Ram Rajya Parishad won between them only 10 Lok Sabha seats in a house of 489, and polled less than six per cent of the vote.'[9] It was a stunning achievement and a fitting tribute to the Indian national movement. Communalism was pushed back for decades.

Now seventy-five years later, we find ourselves once again in a similar situation and are bewildered about how to combat the communal threat to secular democracy in India. In such a situation, let us look back and see what our tallest leaders, Gandhiji and Nehru, did in a similar situation. Their frontal attack on the communal forces and the vision they represented, treating it as the topmost priority to save the Idea of India; their standing openly and bravely with the minorities in independent India, the Muslims particularly, as they were the chief target of the communalists; their refusal to compromise on this question for short-term electoral gains to be garnered from an already communalized people, as happens today; their understanding that without secularism there could not be any democracy in India, are some of the lessons we can learn.[10]

There are several other lessons we can learn from Nehru who was among the first in India to evolve a complex and scientific understanding of communalism, which had to be the first step if one wished to combat it. As he put it, 'The oft repeated appeal for Hindu–Muslim unity, useful as it no doubt is, seemed to me singularly inane, unless some effort was made to understand the causes of the disunity.' In a section called 'Communalism and Reaction' in his Autobiography written during 1934–35[11] and in several other writings and speeches which I shall cite separately, Nehru explores the issue of communalism with great complexity. I will

briefly highlight some of the important generalizations
he made which are relevant even today.

Studying the rise of communalism in India, Nehru
is very clear that it was a *modern* phenomenon, not a
remnant of the medieval past; it did not, for instance,
originate with the arrival of Islam in India. He saw
communalism clearly as a product of the *colonial* period
with active connivance of the colonial state; 'the British
Government . . . throws its sheltering wings over a
useful ally.'[12] In fact, he traces the origin and growth
of communalism with amazing finesse, anticipating
what was confirmed by a lot of scholarly work that has
emerged since.[13] He traces the role of British policy
'since the rising of 1857 . . . of preventing the Hindu
and Muslim from acting together, and of playing off
one community against the other.'[14] He shows how a
number of factors such as the initial heavy discrimination
by the British against Muslims after the 1857 uprising,
seeing them as more dangerous, the lagging behind of
Muslims (as compared to Hindus) in modern education,
in social reform, in evolving a modern intelligentsia and
a Muslim bourgeoisie and particularly lagging behind
in government employment, created a fertile ground
for the evolution of a certain kind of Muslim politics.

A politics, much aided by the colonial government, where an elite, princely, landed section of the Muslims, led by Syed Ahmad Khan, Aga Khan, et al., offered loyalty to the colonial government and opposition to the democratic urges of the emerging Indian national movement against the colonial government. In return, the colonial government granted 'favours' to the 'Muslims' *as a community.* These seeds of communalism sown by British connivance were to grow among other communities over time. He saw that while the communalists, whether Hindu or Muslim, spoke in the name of the community, they actually did not represent the masses of any community but were backed by the vested interests, the feudal aristocracy, landlords, princes and moneylenders who feared the political changes which Indian nationalism ushered in, and consequently supported the existing government.[15] He was able to see that in regions where different economic categories or classes belonged to different religions, the economic conflict 'was given a communal colouring'.

After Independence, in 1952, Nehru added the capitalists among the vested interests supporting communal formations. He said, 'Behind the façade of religion, vested interests, particularly the Zamindars and the *capitalists*, were fighting against the economic policies of the Congress'.[16] Till Independence, the capitalists had, by and large, aligned with the national movement, and not the communal loyalists.[17] With land reforms pushed vigorously after Independence by Nehru, over time the back of the Zamindari forces was broken. As Nehru said in October 1951, 'Jagirdari and zamindari system must go from India . . . The Hindu Mahasabha, Rashtriya Swayamsevak Sangh or the Jan Sangh may thrive on the funds they get from them but there is no power in the world which can perpetuate the system.'[18] With the power of the Zamindari elements much diminished, today we witness the crony *capitalists* performing this role of backing communal forces through funds and control over media on an infinitely larger scale.[19]

Nehru perceptively argued that communalists had nothing to do with religion or with culture and were 'singularly devoid of all ethics and morality', although 'they talk bravely of past culture'[20]. During the first general election of 1951–52, Nehru was severely critical of 'a staunchly communal organization' like the Bharatiya Jan Sangh (the predecessor of the BJP), 'spreading the poison of bitterness and hatred . . . in the name of religion and culture'. He added:

'Generally you will find that those who talk loudly
of Indian culture have really nothing to do with any
culture in the world, Indian or otherwise. Those
who talk of Indian civilization are in fact completely
uncivilized. It is absurd to shout about culture and
civilization from the roof-tops . . . Indian culture
has been so glorious in the past because it has not
followed such communal methods.'[21]

He also noted that though the communalists 'call . . .
themselves non-political', they 'as a matter fact function
politically and their demands are political.'[22] Only their
politics was reactionary and anti-national.

Nehru had realized very early on that his hope that
with the British gone, communalism would disappear
had proved to be unfounded. In the 1930s, he had argued:
'Communalism is essentially a hunt for favour from a
third party—the foreign power . . . *Delete the foreign
power* and communal arguments and demands fall to
the ground'.[23] As we saw above, following Mahatma
Gandhi's assassination, the RSS was banned and around
25,000 RSS activists were put in jail. However, once
the ban was lifted, roughly a year and a half later, in
July 1949, and the prisoners released, the RSS resumed

its ideological offensive. Jawaharlal Nehru repeatedly warned against the dangerous implications of this. In his letters to the chief ministers of the provinces, he said, 'the whole *mentality of the R.S.S. is a fascist mentality.* Therefore, their activities have to be closely watched.'[24] He was very clear and repeatedly said that there was no space for complacency after the spectacular defeat of the communal forces in the first general election. Writing to the presidents of the Provincial Congress Committees, he said in 1952:

'One good thing that has emerged from these elections is our straight fight and success against communalism. That success is significant and heartening. But it is *by no means a complete success* and we have to be wary about this.'[25]

Nehru believed that the first election had taught another significant lesson that there was no percentage in compromising with communalism. A very important lesson in today's context in India. He said:

'We have seen at last that we need not be afraid of communalism and we *need not compromise with it*

as many Congressman did for fear of consequences.
Where we fight it in a straight and honest way, we
win. Where we compromise with it, we lose.'[26]

As early as the 1930s, Nehru had rejected the
warning by friends that his highly critical 'attitude
towards communal organisations will result in
antagonizing many people against' him. He said, 'In
politics people are very careful of what they say and do
not say lest they offend some group or individual and
lose support' but then he was 'yet to learn the ways of
politicians' and 'remain a silent witness' when the nation
was in danger.[27] He therefore refused to compromise
and outright condemned the communal organizations.
An AICC resolution drafted by him in March 1952 read:

'The AICC expresses its deep gratification at the
overwhelming response of the electorate' to the
Congress policy of opposing communalism. 'This
response, however, must not lead Congressman . . .
to think that the danger from communal tendencies
is wholly over. Communal and separatist tendencies
still exist . . . and have to be constantly watched and
combated, whether they are Hindu, Muslim, Sikh

or other . . . the AICC declares that there should be *no alliance, cooperation or understanding, explicit or implicit*, between the Congress and any organization which is essentially communal in character or working.'[28]

In the decades after Nehru, this advice was unfortunately forgotten. In a society already communalized to a considerable extent, the logic of electoral politics led even secular parties of all hues to compromise and resort, in varying degrees, to shortcuts to popular mobilization, by appealing to or allying with parties that appealed to the existing communal consciousness rather than attempting the relatively difficult and long-term task of altering that consciousness.

Nehru led by example in combating the communal forces by both constantly critiquing communal *ideology* and using *state power,* when needed, to do so. He declared on Gandhiji's birth anniversary on 2 October 1951: 'no quarter would be given' to the communal forces and 'as far as he was concerned, he would fight communalism till the last breath of his life both inside and if need be outside the Government.' Hearing the communalists talk of Hindu Rashtra in Delhi and threaten the Muslims to vacate their houses for the incoming refugees and asking them to go to Pakistan, Nehru warned:

> 'if any person raises his hand against another person on basis of religion, *all the resources at the command of the Government will be used* to put him down with an iron hand.'[29]

Aware of the critical role played by the police officials and the district administration in preventing or abetting communal disturbances, including riots, Nehru asked his chief ministers not to accept any excuses 'and put a black mark in the record of every district officer when a communal incident takes place and to inform him of this.'[30]

Communal *ideology* also had to be combatted. Nehru no longer believed, as he did in the 1930s, that once the real economic issues were brought before the masses, the 'communal problem will fade into the background for the masses will be far more interested in filling their hungry stomachs . . .'[31] He argued in October 1951, 'we must put an end to both conscious and unconscious *communal thought* in India. There can be no compromise with that . . . Only then can we realise true freedom and make progress.'[32] He added, 'no amount of economic policies and development projects would be of any use if the people were divided.'[33]

As India's recent history shows, the hope that economic development or growth of economistic class struggles will by itself lead to the erosion of communalism, has been repeatedly belied. Communalism has often spread in economically developed areas and people suffering from hunger have often turned to communalism and communal parties, and not necessarily to class struggle.

Emphasizing the critical importance of an *ideological* battle to challenge the communal onslaught, Nehru told his chief ministers shortly after Independence, when the RSS threat was still very strong: 'Those who are impelled by a faith in a cause can seldom be crushed by superior force. They can only be *defeated by higher idealism* as well as a vision and a capacity to work for the cause that represents these objectives.'[34]

Nehru spoke very strongly against the spreading of the ideology of hate and advocated strong measures against it, even if these measures involved curbing the freedom of the press. While he believed that 'every human being has the right to express his opinion even if it is a criticism against me' and did not 'like the idea of suppressing freedom of expression of newspapers, even if their views are wrong', yet he made an exception. In a long speech delivered from the Ramlila Ground in Delhi on 23 September 1956, shortly before the second general election, Nehru talked of 'the Hindu Mahasabha, Jana Sangh, Rashtriya Swayamsevak Sangh and the Muslim organisations which have now taken the place of the Muslim League and if it is possible for such a thing to happen, are even worse than the Muslim League' who 'rake up religious emotions and incite trouble.' In this context, he said:

'I have been deeply perturbed . . . by the way some newspapers incite violence and spread false rumours and outright lies. Therefore I have reached the conclusion that the newspapers which spread communal hatred and violence should be controlled. I am all in favour of freedom of every kind but if that freedom means rioting and inflaming the people or snatching away the others' freedom or *spreading hatred,* then they should be prevented by law and dealt with strictly . . . We shall not allow communal violence or hatred to be spread, whether it is the Hindus, Muslims or Sikhs or Christians who indulge in such activities . . . I am going to suggest to my . . . Home Minister, Shri Govind Ballabh Pant . . . a law be passed as soon as possible because this situation cannot be tolerated any longer that the newspapers should deliberately spread lies and rumours and create enmity *and make money* out of all this, instead of being punished.'[35]

What a contrast between Nehru as prime minister taking such a stand and the current situation where the press and the visual media are playing a much worse role and the police and administration often collude with the communal forces under the benign gaze of the state, if not its active encouragement! In fact, perhaps the most important factor in the survival and reassertion of the communal forces in India was the fact that the secular forces failed to undertake any sustained ideological work to combat communal ideology, nor were they able to use state power to firmly contain the communal forces. The Hindu communalists, led by the RSS, as well as the minority Sikh and Muslim communalists continued their propaganda, particularly in the education system.

Claiming to be only a 'cultural' organization, the RSS continued to spread their divisive hate ideology, proving Nehru's belief right that the communalists say one thing but do the opposite in practice. The divisive hate ideology was spread through propaganda in the RSS *shakhas*, rumours, newspapers, pamphlets and through a network of educational institutions called the Saraswati Shishu Mandirs, the first of which was started in 1952 in the presence of the RSS Chief M.S. Golwalkar. (The RSS presence in this sensitive sphere has grown phenomenally in the decades after Nehru, particularly when it had access to state power such as during 1977–79, 1999–2004 and 2014 onwards, with the organization looking after education, the Vidya Bharati, claiming on its official website, that in 2022–23, it had 12,065 formal schools with 31,58,658 students and 7797 non-formal schools with 1,88,334 students. It also claimed a reach in *92 per cent of the districts* in India!)[36]

Nothing substantial was done by secular political parties to counter such harmful propaganda either through state action or sustained *anti-communal ideological work* at the ground level. The honourable exception was the effort made in the 1960s through the National Council of Educational Research and Training

(NCERT) to bring to our schoolchildren scientific and secular texts free from communal and colonial prejudices. The tallest of India's historians[37] and other social scientists were persuaded to write textbooks for school children, which remained popular for decades thereafter for their outstanding quality. However, even this effort was gradually snuffed out by the growing communal forces, using state power whenever they got access to it.[38] Ultimately, during the NDA regime led by the BJP (1999–2004), these textbooks were removed and replaced with another set of books. Such was the poor quality of the books and the communal bias in them that the Indian History Congress was constrained to bring out a book in 2003 called *History in the New NCERT Textbooks: A Report and an Index of Errors.* The report concluded: 'Often the errors are apparently mere products of ignorance; but as often they stem from an anxiety to present History with a very strong chauvinistic and communal bias. The textbooks draw heavily on the kind of propaganda that the so called Sangh Parivar publications have been projecting for quite some time.'[39] After 1999, once the communal forces acquired state power at the national level, they used it to rapidly spread communalism through the education system and other means which, it has been argued, contributed to one of the worst pogroms in Indian history since Independence, the Gujarat carnage of 2002.[40] When the secular intelligentsia, including some of the tallest intellectuals of the country, tried to resist the saffronization of education, and particularly the discipline of history,[41] they were branded as 'anti-Hindu Euro Indians'.[42] More ominously, eminent historians who had resisted the attempt at communalization were accused of 'intellectual terrorism' which was 'more dangerous than cross border terrorism' by the BJP education minister![43]

The communal forces were pushed back in 2004 and the secular forces, led by the Congress, came back to power, with the slogan of secularizing education and of 'de-Talibanising' it. However, in the ten long years that they were in power from 2004 to 2014, unfortunately not enough was done on this front. Though the NCERT textbooks brought out during the BJP regime (1999–2004) were replaced with secular and scientific texts written by a number of eminent scholars from all over the country, no effort was made to prevent virulently communal texts such as those brought out by the RSS[44] from continuing to be taught in a large number of RSS schools. The ideological battle against communalism was not taken up on a war footing by the secular forces. Their record in being able to use state power to bring to book those complicit in the Gujarat tragedy was equally dismal. As a result, since 2014, once again the NCERT texts are being communalized and the relentless targeting of the minorities, particularly the Muslims, has resumed.[45]

There are a few more important lessons to be learnt from Nehru on the issue of communalism.

Since the 1930s, Nehru had made a subtle distinction between minority and majority communalism. Nehru was empathetic to the minority condition and their fears when he said, 'Honest communalism is fear; false communalism is reaction. To some extent this fear is justified, or is at least understandable, in a minority community. We see this fear overshadowing the communal sky in India as a whole so far as Muslims are concerned; we see it as an equally potent force in the Punjab and Sind so far as the Hindus are concerned, and in the Punjab, the Sikhs.' The colonial state, he said, stoked these fears and pulled the minority communalists towards loyalism.

While criticizing minority communalism, Nehru felt that there was a need for the majority to allay the fears of the minority, rather than exacerbate these fears. The founding fathers of the Indian national movement and those of the Indian National Congress had, since its inception, adopted this approach. The Hindu communalists then, as they do now, saw this as a policy of *'appeasement'* of the minorities and adopted a stance which worsened matters. As Nehru argued: 'A special *responsibility* does attach to the Hindus in India both because they are the majority community and because economically and educationally they are more advanced.' However, 'the (Hindu) Mahasabha, instead of discharging that responsibility, has acted in a manner which has undoubtedly increased the communalism of the Muslims and made them distrust the Hindus all the more. The only way it has tried to meet their communalism is by its own variety of communalism.' Nehru then goes on to make the classic statement which should be the mantra of all secularists:

'One communalism does not end the other; *each feeds on the other and both fatten.*'[46]

In fact, he pointed out very early in the 1930s the phenomenon that while 'the Hindu and the Muslim communalists attack each other in public they cooperate in the Assembly and elsewhere in helping Government to pass reactionary measures.'[47] After all, the Muslim League and the Hindu Mahasabha joined hands to form governments in Sind and the North West Frontier Provinces and cooperated with the government while the Congress had resigned from provincial governments in protest against the British imperialist policy in 1939. In fact, as the Congress resigned, the Muslim League, true to its loyalist character, offered cooperation to form the government. Not to be outdone, Savarkar, then the president of the Hindu Mahasabha, told the Viceroy in October 1939 that the Hindus and the British should be friends and made an offer that the Hindu Mahasabha would replace the Congress if the Congress ministries resigned from office.[48] Shyama Prasad Mookerjee, the Hindu Mahasabha leader (later one of the founders of the Bharatiya Jan Sangh), was a minister in the Bengal government led by Fazlul Haq, who had moved the Pakistan Resolution at the Muslim League session in 1940. The communalists were cooperating with the British at a time when they brutally suppressed the Congress as it launched the 1942 Quit India movement. This phenomenon has continued over the decades till today. After all, the chief enemy of the communal forces is the secular forces as they question their *raison d'etre* while the communalism of the 'other' helps them grow even more or 'fatten'.

While understanding the 'fears' that help the growth of minority communalism, it did not lead Nehru to be soft towards, leave alone support, minority communalism. When he was 'chided for not blaming Muslim communalists' while making a strong critique of the Hindu communalism of the Hindu Sabha in a speech delivered at the Banaras Hindu University on 12 November 1933, at the invitation of Vice Chancellor Madan Mohan Malaviya (who incidentally was one of the early leaders of the Sabha), Nehru made a very important point: the need to critique the communalism of the audience one is addressing. He said, 'it would have been entirely out of place for me, speaking to a Hindu audience, to draw attention to Muslim communalists and reactionaries. It would have been preaching to the converted as the average Hindu is well aware of them. It is far more difficult to see one's own fault than to see the failing of others.'[49] The critiquing of the communalism of the other community, rather than the one being addressed, is easy and can even amount to pandering to the communalism of the audience. An important lesson even today.

Nehru, in fact, was as critical of minority communalism as he was of majority communalism; he believed that 'there is no essential difference between the two'.[50] He had no hesitation in describing Muslim League leaders and Muslim communalists as loyalists, 'definitely anti-national and political reactionaries of the worst kind.'[51] A lesson to be learnt here as there has been a tendency, in the years after Independence, on the part of certain secular forces to exhibit a softness towards minority communalism, or towards the parties that took the support of minority communalists, often on the plea that they were relatively backward or were being discriminated against by the majority community. This tendency was exhibited even by sections of the Left. This was one of the major factors in enabling the majority communalists to extend their influence. A heavy price was paid for ignoring the sage advice given by Jawaharlal Nehru referred to earlier, that 'one communalism does not end the other; each feeds on the other and both fatten.' Softness towards minority communalism made the growth of majority communalism much easier.

Interestingly, in contrast to the Hindu communal critique of Nehru being soft on minority communalism and appeasing them, Nehru and the Indian nationalist leadership was also accused of the opposite. Somewhat in line with the *colonial* position, they were accused of *not* being sensitive to and of accommodating minority/ Muslim demands, such as the separate electorates, and hence pushing the country towards a bloody Partition. This old view has been repeated recently, by some Eurocentric Marxists like Perry Anderson,[52] and surprisingly by an admirer and fine scholar of Nehru in many other aspects, Manash Firaq Bhattacharjee, whom I have referred to appreciatively above. He says, 'The possibility that the fear of the minority against majoritarianism may be real doesn't occur to Nehru'. Also, he sees the nationalist critique of minority identity politics in a 'communal/national binary' as problematic and says it has 'an anti-minoritarian streak . . . that can be termed *secular majoritarianism.*' He says, 'To pit communalism against nationalism is a Nehruvian error.' Bhattacharjee grossly misreads the ideology and the actual history of the Indian national movement when he sees the nationalists as seeing *only minority identity politics* as 'communal', emerging 'surreptitiously' from a 'majoritarian reluctance to share power'.[53]

The tallest leaders of the Indian national movement, led by Gandhiji and Nehru, put their lives at stake to protect minority rights and enable the religious minorities to have equal citizenship rights in the Indian republic, but refused to do so by pandering to minority identity politics as it would stand against the whole republican idea of citizenship. It is an absolute canard to describe the Indian nationalist position as *'secular majoritarianism'* with 'an anti-minoritarian streak (since the late 1920s)', as Bhattacharjee does. The national movement was correct in erecting a 'communal/national' binary. Communal politics *by definition* broke up the 'nation' in a multireligious country. That is why the colonial state constantly encouraged and supported communalism of all varieties and it is a historical fact that the communal forces who engaged in politics of religious identity, whether they be of minority or majority, allied with the colonial state and saw the Congress, which spoke of a nation where religion would not determine politics, as the chief enemy. Empowering politics based on religion was the colonial project and could not be that of the nationalists and ought not be that of such a fine scholar of Nehru as Bhattacharjee, or Eurocentric Marxists like Perry Anderson.

Apart from completely missing Nehru's subtle understanding of minority fears while opposing minority communalism (discussed above), the portrayal of Nehru as 'Majoritarian' is a total travesty. If it were true, the Hindu majoritarians would not have seen him as such an impediment to the success of their project and thus would not have needed to demonize him in the manner they have done. In fact, a more ardent critic of majoritarian, Hindu communalism in India would be difficult to find. In 1933, he said:

'The policy of the Hindu Mahasabha . . . is one of cooperation with the foreign government so that, by abasing themselves before it, they might get a few crumbs. This is a betrayal of the freedom struggle, *denial of every vestige of nationalism*, suppressive of every manly instinct in the Hindus . . . Anything more degrading, reactionary, *anti-national,* anti-progressive and harmful than the policy of the Hindu Mahasabha is difficult to imagine'.[54]

So much for Nehru's so-called 'secular majoritarian' streak.

It is also to be noted that Nehru was also among the first to emphasize that majority communalism easily 'masquerades under a *nationalist* cloak'.[55] Minority communalism on the other hand 'grew and fed itself . . . on *separatism*'.[56] He said, 'It must be remembered that the communalism of a majority community must of necessity bear a closer resemblance to nationalism than the communalism of the minority . . . "*Hindu Nationalism*" . . . is but another name for communalism'.[57] Nehru, therefore, categorically reiterates that the Hindu communal organizations may call themselves nationalist but are in reality '*anti-national* and reactionary'.[58]

The current type of masculine, aggressive, alpha-male nationalism that is being paraded around by Hindutva forces was squarely characterized by Nehru and the Indian national movement as 'anti-national.' It is important to remind ourselves of this as there has been a gradual ceding of the *nationalist space* by the secular forces which has contributed a great deal to enabling communalists, who were pro-colonial and thereby played an anti-national role when the Indian people were struggling for freedom, to successfully masquerade today as the real nationalists and garner the tremendous mass appeal that the nationalist sentiment commands.

The very acceptance of the self-description of the majority communalists as *'Hindu Nationalists'* is a grave error. During the entire national movement for Independence, they were called communalists, *not* Hindu nationalists, as it was so obviously a contradiction in terms; by restricting nation to the Hindus, the others were left out, thus dividing the nation itself. But the phrase gained currency among foreign journalists, commentators and academics[59] writing for foreign audiences unfamiliar with the meaning of the term 'communalism' as used in the Indian context and is now unfortunately routinely used by Indian analysts and journalists.

The secular forces have made it easier for the communalists to occupy the nationalist space by themselves neglecting, critiquing and even *ridiculing,* the national liberation struggle and its tallest leaders. The condemning of Gandhiji, Nehru, Patel, Tilak, Aurobindo as communal or semi-communal, with a 'majoritarian' streak, the branding of the national movement as bourgeois, and its leaders as agents of the bourgeoisie, if not of imperialism itself, or as upper caste leaders fighting for their respective groups rather than representing the people of the country, etc., was done by secular ideologues, including those from the Left, such as Perry Anderson most recently.[60] The need, on the other hand, was to first own up the ancestry and the great legacy of the Indian national movement, one of the most powerful national liberation struggles in the world, and then, standing on its shoulders, build upon it by making advances, going beyond the breakthroughs made by that struggle. Its rejection simply made it easy for the communalists to *appropriate* its legacy. Witness the attempt to appropriate Gandhi, Patel, Tilak, Aurobindo, Bhagat Singh, Subhas Chandra Bose, etc., by the majoritarian communal forces while each one of them were deeply secular. Nehru was spared this ignominy, perhaps as he was seen as too sharp a critic of communalism to be appropriated. Also, with the untimely end of Bhagat Singh and Bose, Gandhiji's assassination and Patel passing away soon after, it was Nehru who remained the most prominent steadfast critic of the communal forces.

Finally, a major contribution of Nehru was to repeatedly warn of the *fascist* nature of communalism. As Bipan Chandra wrote: 'Nehru was . . . the first to see communalism as a form of fascism. Before 1947, he saw the close resemblance between the post-1937 Muslim League and fascism both in terms of methods, techniques of hatred and violence, organization and style of leadership and in terms of language and ideology. After 1947, he began to apply this understanding to Hindu and Sikh communalism, especially to the Rashtriya Swayamsevak Sangh (RSS).'[61] In December 1947, a few months before the assassination of the Mahatma, Nehru as prime minister warned the chief ministers: 'We have a great deal of evidence to show the R.S.S. is an organization which is in the nature of a private army and which is definitely proceeding on the *strictest Nazi lines,* even following the technique of organization.'[62] Even after the ban on the RSS, following Gandhiji's murder, was lifted, in 1949, following a written assurance that they would not engage in politics and remain only a cultural organization, Nehru warned the chief ministers: 'Reports reach us that the R.S.S. is again resuming some of its activities . . . But it must always be remembered that the whole *mentality of the R.S.S. is a fascist mentality.* Therefore, their activities have to be closely watched.'[63] He warned:

'Communalism bears a striking resemblance to the various forms of fascism that we have seen in other countries. *It is in fact the Indian version of fascism* . . . It plays upon the basest instincts of man.'[64]

On another occasion, he said, 'Communalism was *diametrically opposed to democracy* and usually relied on Nazi and Fascist methods'.[65] In a public speech in Delhi on 2 October 1951, while warning against the various aspects of communalism, he said, '*Communalism . . . I call it by another name—fascism*', by following this path 'ultimately the result would be similar to what happened to Hitler and fascism in Europe. I do not want India to follow that terrible path'.[66]

Despite all these early warnings, what we are witnessing is the playing out of the fascist threat in India. Having acquired *governmental* power with an absolute majority since 2014, the Hindu communalists found that India was still not a Hindu *state* or Hindu Rashtra. The effort, therefore, now was to change the character of the Indian state from a secular state to a Hindu state. This involved not only acquiring governmental power, but also changing the character of all the state apparatuses and changing the mindset of the people, of civil society at large. All of them had to be communalized. This in turn involved control over the bureaucracy, police, judiciary, media, the education system and the containment of free speech and civil liberties. It also involves the withdrawal of the civil rights of the religious minorities and shutting out their voices as well as of those who try to speak up for them. All this could not be achieved without the use of coercion and force, and even violence. The regime therefore began to take on a fascist character, or as Prabhat Patnaik put it 'Fascism arrives in camouflage'.[67]

In a very recent article for *The Guardian,* Jason Stanley, philosopher at Yale University and the author of the celebrated work, *How Fascism Works,*[68] voices a scathing critique of the current situation in India. A brief extract is in order:

'The hallmarks of fascism are everywhere. *School textbooks are being rewritten to reinforce the fake history behind BJP's Hindu nationalist agenda.* Topics like the theory of evolution and the periodic table have been replaced with traditional Hindu theories, and academics have been silenced for calling out the BJP's election malpractices. The government has weaponized education in the manner typical of fascist regimes . . . There are other clear indications of India's slide towards fascism. On press freedom, India ranks 161st out of 180 countries, sandwiched between Venezuela (at 159) and Russia (at 164) . . . India's minorities face lynchings and the bulldozing of their homes, among other abuses. Ten percent of the world's Muslims live in India, over 200 million in all; as Gregory Stanton, the founder and director of Genocide Watch, has warned in a US congressional briefing, *we are seeing in India the beginning of what would be by far the largest genocide in history.*'[69]

The bulldozer appears to have become the frightening imagery as well as the reality of punishing the minorities. A recent 'bulldozing' of the minorities was done right next to the capital, Delhi, in August 2023, following a deliberately provoked conflict in the Mewat region.[70] The Punjab and Haryana High Court was constrained to take *suo moto* action, intervening against the reported targeted bulldozing of the properties of the Muslim minority, saying that the issue arises 'whether the buildings belonging to a particular community are being brought down under the guise of law and order problem and an exercise of *ethnic cleansing* is being *conducted by the state.*'[71]

Faced with a similar communal upheaval, Nehru had some advice for the way ahead from which we may learn. A winning of an election, arrest of a few and banning of certain organizations may be the first step ahead but it was not going to be enough. Addressing lakhs of people shortly after the murder of the Mahatma by a communalist, he said: 'The Government have arrested some persons and put them in jails and have declared two or three organisations unlawful. If by these actions . . . it is thought that the whole thing is over then people are mistaken. *We have to uproot this despicable communalism. It must be obliterated from this land so that it may not take roots again.* This poison has . . . permeated the land.'[72]

This poison had to be fought, as we saw above, not only with 'superior force' but with a 'higher idealism'. The 'higher idealism' that Nehru and the leaders of his time offered was a humane, inclusive *nationalism* and a democratic socialism.

Building
Democracy

The threat to Indian democracy posed by communalism, or by *'communal fascism,'* as Amartya Sen, perhaps first, described it,[1] is now perceived globally. Michelguglielmo Torri, arguably the foremost Italian scholar on India, has outlined the rapid growth in recent years of the forces trying to transform India's secular democracy into a Hindu State (Rashtra) and the repressive authoritarian manner in which it is being done, leading to a situation where he says India can no longer be called a full democracy.[2] In fact, international bodies such as the V-Dem Institute of Sweden, the US-based Freedom House, and *The Economist*'s EIU (Economist Intelligence Unit), which produces the Democracy Index, are no longer accepting India as a full democracy. 'A democratic backsliding' is said to be occurring and India is being variously described as 'a partially free democracy', 'a flawed democracy' or even 'an electoral autocracy'. The downgrading was based on what was perceived as the current regime promoting anti-minority feeling and legislation, the violation of human rights with 'the diminishing of freedom of expression, the media and civil society hav(ing) gone the furthest'.[3] Rather than engaging with this downgrading and seeking to introspect, the government and its supporters are trying to create a counter-narrative that this downgrading is Western bias at work.[4]

How far we have moved from Nehru's dream! What can we learn from Nehru?

For Jawaharlal Nehru, democracy and civil liberties were absolute values, which could not be compromised for any goal, however laudable, be it planning, economic development or social justice. This had a critical impact on how these other goals were sought to be achieved. 'I would not,' declared Nehru, 'give up the democratic system *for anything*.'[5] In this, he was reflecting faith in a non-negotiable core of the Indian national movement, democracy and civil liberties, best expressed by Mahatma Gandhi in his inimitable idiom: 'Civil liberty *consistent with the observance of non-violence* . . . is the foundation of freedom. *There is no room there for dilution or compromise.* It is the water of life. I have never heard of water being diluted.'[6]

The 1931 Karachi Resolution of the Congress, which formed the basic kernel of the future Constitution of India, and was drafted by Nehru and moved by

Gandhiji, had as its first item: 'Every citizen of India has the right to free expression of opinion, the right of free association and combination, and the right to assemble peacefully and without arms.'[7] Nehru was 'the strongest force behind founding the Indian Civil Liberties Union in 1936 as a non-party, non-sectarian organisation.'[8] Nehru persuaded Rabindranath Tagore to become the honorary president of the Indian Civil Liberties Union and Sarojini Naidu to become the functioning chairperson, and actively encouraged the formation of several such unions in the provinces.[9]

Freedom of the press was an essential aspect of civil liberty. Defining what he meant by the freedom of the press, Nehru said in 1940:

'The freedom of the press does not consist in our permitting such things as we like to appear. Even a tyrant is agreeable to this kind of freedom. Civil liberty and freedom of press consist in our permitting what we do not like, in our putting up with criticism of ourselves . . .'[10]

Nehru's commitment to a free press was absolute and remained as strong when he was in government as it was when he was leading the struggle against the colonial state. No cartoonist had to go to jail in his times, nor did stand-up comedians or journalists before they performed or were yet to write a story!

Apart from seeing democracy and civil liberty as essential values in themselves, Nehru strongly believed that a country as diverse as India could be held together only by a non-violent, democratic way of life, and not by force or coercion. Only a democratic structure that gave space to various linguistic, religious, cultural, political and socio-economic trends to express themselves could hold India together. Almost as if anticipating the danger faced by the nation today, he said:

'This is too large a country with too many legitimate diversities to *permit any so-called "strong man"* to trample over people and their ideas.'[11]

He was careful not to allow himself to fall prey to populism or plebiscitary/majoritarian democracy at a time when he, after Gandhiji's and Patel's death, towered over the Indian political spectrum and could easily have smothered opposition to himself and his policies. He correctly saw that the heart of democracy lay in respecting difference of opinion, even if it be that of a minority. He said on 2 June 1950, before the first general elections:

'I am not afraid of the opposition in this country and I do not mind if opposition groups grow up on the basis of some theory, practice or constructive theme. I do not want India to be a country in which millions of people say 'yes' to one man, *I want a strong opposition*.'[12]

A telling example of Nehru respecting opposition and his conviction that India should not countenance any tendency towards the emergence of a 'dictator' or any one 'strong man', was a critique he wrote of himself under a pseudonym at a time when he was at the peak of his popularity. It was as if he was warning himself and the Indian people at large against any such tendency emerging in himself and in Indian politics! Elected president of the Indian National Congress for two consecutive years, he wrote an article (using the pseudonym, Chanakya) titled 'Rashtrapati' or 'President' in a popular journal in October 1937, warning:

'Men like Jawaharlal with all their capacity for great and good work, are unsafe in a democracy . . . A little twist and Jawaharlal might turn a dictator sweeping aside the paraphernalia of a slow-moving democracy. He might still use the language and slogan of democracy and socialism, but we all know how *fascism* has fattened on this language . . . He has all the makings of a dictator in him—vast popularity, a strong will directed to a well-defined purpose, energy, pride, organisational capacity, ability, hardness and with all his love of the crowd, an intolerance of others and a certain contempt for the weak and the inefficient . . . His over-mastering desire to get things done, to sweep away what he dislikes and build anew, will hardly brook for long the slow process of democracy . . . Caesarism is always at the door, and is it not possible that Jawaharlal might fancy himself as a Caesar?'[13]

Nehru was warning himself and his people against any compromises with democracy and civil liberty. While he succeeded in great measure in sticking scrupulously to the democratic path and in making the democratic path a part of the common sense of the Indian people, the dangers he was alluding to have not lost their salience for India today, sixty years after the end of the Nehru era.

Now, unfortunately, 'Mukti' (freedom) from any opposition is declared as the goal; Congress mukt (free of Congress), 'Lutyens Delhi' mukt, Left-liberal mukt, *andolanjeevi/parjeevi* (agitationists/parasites) mukt, independently thinking universities like JNU mukt, NGOs mukt, Amnesty International India mukt, Human Rights Organizations mukt, are some examples of what 'Bharat' must be mukt of!

Apart from nurturing a robust opposition through a free expression of ideas by an independent media, Nehru also paid a great deal of attention to other critical institutions of a functional democracy, such as the parliament. The respect he gave to the parliament and parliamentary practice and code of conduct, right up to his death, was legendary and could be an object lesson to our present parliamentarians. He patiently sat through long sessions in parliament, even when ill, and personally answered each question and criticism. He never silenced the opposition even when he was under vicious attack, for example on the Kashmir issue and on the 1962 China debacle. He patiently answered each criticism both inside parliament and outside. Witness, for example, his long and patient response to the criticism of his policies by Shyama Prasad Mookerjee.[14] Atal Bihari Vajpayee, a leader of the Jana Sangh, which was the main party of Hindu communalism and vehemently opposed to Nehru, and who was later the prime minister of India from 1998 to 2004, had found words of praise from Nehru for his robust opposition. Vajpayee, in his tribute to Nehru on his passing away said,

> 'The loss to parliament is irreparable. Such a resident may never grace Teen Murti (the residence of the Prime Minister) again. That vibrant personality, that attitude of *taking even the opposition along,* that refined gentlemanliness, that greatness we may not again see in the near future. In spite of difference of opinion we have nothing but respect for his great ideals, his integrity, his love for the country and his indomitable courage.'[15]

Comparisons with today's situation are self-evident. Nehru took great care to institutionalize the cabinet system of government. Not only did he not usurp all powers to himself, he refused to give in to the tendency among many of his colleagues to leave important policy decisions to him. C.D. Deshmukh, who was finance minister in Nehru's cabinet from 1950 to 1956, recorded in his autobiography that 'Nehru as head of the cabinet was gentle, considerate and democratic, never forcing a decision on his colleagues . . .'[16]

Nehru was very careful in trying to build democratic institutions with as little interference from the state as possible, whether it be the judiciary, bureaucracy or other institutions. This was particularly true of *academic institutions* which are critical to a functioning democracy. He said in December 1947:

'A university stands for humanism. For tolerance, for reason, for the adventure of ideas and the search for truth . . . If universities discharge their duty adequately, then it is well with the nation and the people. But if the temple of learning itself becomes a home of narrow bigotry and petty objectives, how, then, will a nation prosper or a people grow in stature?'[17]

Some of the finest institutions were created and nurtured in his time. My university, Jawaharlal Nehru University (JNU), which was set up a few years after Nehru passed away, has tried, since its inception, to institutionalize Nehruvian ideas of fearless independent thought, a scientific and secular ethos and equal opportunity for all, taking into account disabilities emerging from caste, class and regional backwardness.[18] It tried to follow Nehru's idea of a university and inscribed part of the passage quoted above under his statue erected in a prominent space in the campus. However, JNU and several educational institutions of great repute are struggling to survive the current assault on them where 'the adventure of ideas' and dissent is suppressed, often brutally. Students are beaten up, arrested and put in jail for years and even denied bail, faculty is intimidated, and efforts are made to alter syllabi to suit the government's communal bias. JNU, which ranked repeatedly, including by the Government, as the top university in the country, was demonized, particularly since 2016, using a pliant media spreading lies and doctored evidence, as a university promoting terrorists, anti-nationals, the *tukre-tukre gang* (those who profess breaking up of the country), etc., so much so that autos and taxis would often refuse to bring passengers to the campus![19] The 'temple of learning' is indeed becoming a 'home of narrow bigotry.'

Almost all the institutions of democracy so carefully nurtured by Nehru are under severe threat today.

Economic Development with Democracy and Sovereignty

If maintenance of sovereignty and democracy with civil liberty were two non-negotiables bequeathed to independent India by the Indian national movement, then all efforts at post-colonial transformation in India would have had to occur within these parameters. However, never before in history was the process of transition to industrialism or the process of primitive accumulation of capital accomplished along with democracy. The Nehruvian attempt at industrial transformation *with democracy* was thus a *unique* attempt. Nehru was deeply conscious of this and often spoke about it being an uncharted path, '*unique in history*'.[1]

The non-negotiable commitment to democracy meant that the necessary 'surplus' required for investment in order to facilitate the transition to industrialism could not be raised *forcibly* on the backs of the Indian working class and peasantry or on the basis of colonial surplus appropriation as had happened in other countries in the past.[2] Nehruvian state intervention and planning was to be *consensual* and not a *command* performance. The path of extracting surplus out of agriculture through 'expropriatory' land tax or forced collectivization; of forcing surplus out of labour though slavery, indentured labour and in the absence of organized trade union rights or of forcing surplus out of the people of other countries through collection of tribute from colonies, was not open to India. While, during colonial rule, the Indian peasant often ended up handing over more than half of his gross produce as land tax and rent, after Independence, a democratic regime based on popular will meant that not only was there no tax, or surplus extraction through other forms from agriculture (on which an overwhelming majority of the Indian people were dependent), but a net transfer of income to agriculture occurred through state subsidies. Also, trade union rights to the working class were guaranteed from the very beginning and were exercised vigorously. Of course, the question of appropriating colonial tribute from other countries did not even arise. In fact, even after Indian Independence, Nehru remained a relentless champion of liberation movements against imperialist domination in other parts of the world.

Similarly, the non-negotiable commitment to sovereignty meant that the transition to modernity could not be accomplished with foreign aid, foreign capital or foreign intervention in any manner that would make India a junior partner of any advanced country, however powerful it may be. The imperative of maintaining sovereignty was a natural pointer towards the Nehruvian non-alignment policy in the post-Second World War Cold War situation where the world was sought to be divided into two power blocs.

Industrial Transformation and Overall Growth

Nehru and the early Indian planners had correctly understood that political Independence was of little value if it could not be used to acquire first economic and then intellectual Independence. In a special letter to the chief ministers in 1949, he warned them, 'in any real sense of the word this fight for freedom is not over, though we may be politically free. It is not over in the economic sense . . .'[3] At Independence, because of the colonial structuring of the Indian economy, India was almost completely dependent on the advanced world for capital goods and technology for making any investment. It produced virtually no capital goods. In 1950, India met nearly 90 per cent of its needs of machines and *even machine tools* through imports. This meant that despite political Independence, it was completely dependent on the advanced countries for achieving *any* economic growth through investment.

This was a neo-colonial type of situation, which needed immediate remedy. This is what the famous Nehru–Mahalanobis strategy tried to reverse by adopting a heavy industry or capital-goods industry based industrialization. During the first three Five Year plans (1951–65), industry in India grew at 7.1 per cent per annum. This was a far cry from the de-industrialization process of the 19th century and the slow industrial growth between 1914–47. More important, 'the *three-fold* increase in aggregate index of industrial production between 1951 and 1969 was the result of a 70 per cent increase in consumer goods industries, a *quadrupling* of the intermediate goods production and a *ten-fold* increase in the output of capital goods.'[4] This pattern of industrial development led to a *structural transformation* of the colonial legacy. From a situation where, to make any capital investment in India, virtually the entire equipment (90 per cent) had to be imported, the share of imported equipment in the total fixed investment in the form of equipment had come down to 43 per cent in 1960 and a mere 9 per cent in 1974, whereas the value of the fixed investment in India increased by about two and a half times over the period (1960–74).[5]

This was a major achievement towards self-reliance, and it considerably increased India's autonomy from the advanced countries in determining her own rate of capital accumulation or growth. It thus created the key condition for non-alignment or relative Independence from both the power blocs. In my understanding, no amount of diplomatic finesse could achieve and sustain the objective of non-alignment without the economic basis of relative autonomy having been created. It was this un-structuring of the colonial structure which was to later enable India to participate in the globalization process with considerable advantage to itself. The policy of non-alignment, in other words, was as much a function of the strategy of economic development chosen by India, as it was a product of the Indian national movement's commitment to world peace and the sovereignty of nation states. Conversely, non-alignment became a viable strategy only as India began to gain economic sovereignty.

As India, at Independence, did not have a sufficiently large indigenous private sector to take on the massive task of developing capital goods industries, the only other option was to develop it through the public sector. The option of basing the development of this sector on foreign capital did not arise as the Nehruvian consensus was that sovereignty would be achieved only if its industrial development was primarily built indigenously, and was not based on foreign capital. The public sector was clearly seen, by a wide spectrum of opinion, which *included the capitalists* and the Left, as the alternative to foreign capital domination.[6] The public sector soon transformed the industrial and infrastructural landscape in India. In Nehru's time, four major steel plants at Rourkela, Bhilai, Durgapur and Bokaro came up in the public sector. A large number of capital goods industries, infrastructure projects and other areas, requiring large investments, which the Indian private sector could not have developed at that time, were started in the public sector. To list just a few, Indian Telephone Industries, Bhakra Dam, Damodar Valley Corporation and the Hirakud Dam were started in 1947–48 itself; Hindustan

Machine Tools (HMT), Bharat Heavy Electricals Limited, Hindustan Shipyard, Bharat Petroleum, Heavy Engineering Corporation, Indian Oil Corporation, Hindustan Antibiotics, Hindustan Insecticides, Nagarjuna Sagar Dam, National Mineral Development Corporation were started in the 1950s and National Building and Construction Corporation, Indian Drugs and Pharmaceuticals Limited, Fertiliser Corporation of India, Shipping Corporation of India, Hindustan Aeronautics Limited, Bharat Earth Movers were started in the early 1960s.

It is important to point out that, in Nehru's time, these public sector undertakings were *not* loss making 'white elephants' acting as a drag on national resources, which some of them ended up becoming in later decades. On the contrary, they *contributed* to resource mobilization in India, apart from creating self-reliance in critical areas. Public sector savings were throughout the Nehruvian period from 1950–51 to 1964–65, *considerably higher* than that of the private corporate sector.[7] Nehru could proudly announce, while inaugurating the second HMT factory in 1961, that 'this factory has been made out of the profits or the surplus of the older Hindustan Machine Tools factory.'[8] Today's neoliberals who push for indiscriminate privatization totally ignore this aspect.

While reducing the dependence on foreign capital and technology for making indigenous investment was one way of gaining and keeping the country's sovereignty intact, other strategies were adopted as well. India undertook a deliberate strategy of diversifying its foreign trade so that her dependence on any one country or bloc of countries was reduced. As a result, the geographical concentration index (GCI) of trade with foreign countries declined sharply. The GCI of India's exports declined from 0.69 in 1947 to 0.22 in 1975. There was a similar decline in GCI in the case of imports. Significantly, the result of the declining GCI was that the share of the metropolitan countries of the West, which earlier dominated India's trade, declined sharply. For example, the share of the UK and the US in India's exports, which was 45 per cent in 1947, fell by more than half, and by 1977, it was only 20 per cent.[9] This was partly achieved by the increase in India's trade with the Socialist bloc (which bailed India out at a time when she was extremely short of foreign exchange by allowing barter and Rupee trade) and other underdeveloped countries.

In recent years, however, there has been a growing tendency, particularly among neo-colonial scholars like Tirthankar Roy and Meghnad Desai, to dismiss or run down the economic achievements of the Nehruvian era. Looking back from the vantage point of the high growth rates since the economic reforms of 1991, the Nehru years are described as a wasted opportunity. The strategy of trying to reverse the colonial structuring of the Indian economy through a mixed economy with a substantial public sector and an inward oriented, import substituting self-reliant growth, which involved protecting the fledgling domestic industry, was seen as the main problem.[10] As Meghnad Desai put it, 'The first 40 years of India's Independence were wasted.'[11]

This assessment is completely ahistorical. It is oblivious of the massive increase in all the indicators of growth, per capita GDP, industry, agriculture, savings, investment or domestic capital formation that occurred in the Nehruvian period, as compared to the colonial times. Also, it ignores the fact that the growth parameters in Nehru's time compared extremely favourably when compared to other countries of the world at the same stage of development, including the UK, USA, France, China and Japan. While I have done a detailed comparison of the growth parameters in Nehru's time after Independence with the colonial period as well as with other countries at a comparative stage elsewhere,[12] I will give here some indicators.

India's national income or Gross National Product (GNP) grew at an average rate of about 4 per cent per annum, between 1951 and 1964–65, excluding the last year of the Third Plan, i.e., 1965–66, which saw an unprecedented drought and a war. This was roughly *four times* the rate of growth achieved during the last half century of colonial rule. The rate of growth achieved by India after Independence compared favourably with the rates achieved by the advanced countries at a comparable stage, i.e., during their early development. To quote eminent economist Professor K.N. Raj:-

'Japan is generally believed to be a country which grew rapidly in the latter part of the 19th and the first quarter of the 20th century; yet the rate of growth of national income in Japan was slightly less than 3 per cent per annum in the period 1893–1912 and did not go up to more than 4 per cent per annum even in the following decade. Judged by criteria such as these the growth rate achieved

in India in the last decade and a half (1950–65) is
certainly a matter for some satisfaction.'[13]

More important, a similar impressive growth of *per
capita income* also occurs in India. In the colonial period,
the growth of per capita income was either zero or very
low, remaining way below that of the independent
countries of Europe, USA and Japan between 1820 and
1913. In the last decades of colonial rule after colonialism
had had its full impact, the per capita income in India
actually *declined* at an annual rate of 0.22 per cent
between 1913–50.[14] After Independence, on the other
hand, it grew annually at 1.4 per cent in the first couple
of decades (about three times faster than the *best* phase,
1870–1913, under colonialism). The un-structuring of
colonialism in the initial decades after Independence laid
the basis for much faster growth of *per capita income*,
at 3.01 per cent annually in the next thirty years, 1973–
2001 (a rate considerably higher than that achieved by
West Europe,[15] USA or Japan) and between 2003–04
to 2006–07 at an astounding 7 per cent (it was over 8
per cent in 2006–07), comparable to the explosive rates
achieved by Japan (though in very special circumstances)
between 1950–73.[16]

The rate of capital formation, the key to economic development, occurred at a very slow pace during the colonial period. India was in fact losing to Britain as drain or tribute an equal proportion, if not more, of what was invested in India. The drain from India has been variously calculated to be between 5 and 10 per cent of her national income.[17] In fact, if one pitted outflows on current account due to interest, dividends and home charges against the net inflow due to foreign borrowing on the capital account, one would find that there was an outflow of capital from India virtually throughout the colonial period and certainly since the First World War.[18] Even if we ignore the colonial capital appropriation, what the early nationalists called the drain, we find that for the last fifty years or so of colonial rule (1901–46) the gross capital formation in the economy hovered around 6 to 7 per cent of GDP annually, while the first fifty years after Independence saw the rate of capital formation rise consistently and sharply. It was double the colonial rate between 1955 and 1970, ending up at a rate of 33.8 per cent in 2005–06, about *five times* the colonial rate.[19]

There was also a rapid *per capita* increase in the availability of some of the infrastructural and social benefits as they grew several times faster than the population immediately after Independence. In 1965–66, as compared to 1950–51, the installed capacity of electricity was 4.5 times higher, the number of towns and villages electrified was fourteen times higher, the number of hospital beds was 2.5 times higher, enrolment in schools was a little less than three times higher and, very importantly, the admission capacity in technical education (engineering and technology) at the degree and diploma levels was higher by six and 8.5 times, respectively. This when the population increased only by 37.3 per cent over the period.[20]

The neo-colonial, neoliberal critics of Nehru, like Tirthankar Roy and Meghnad Desai, ignore this major breakthrough that took place after Independence, which resulted in the structural transformation of the colonial economy that was inherited. Also, they fail to see the global structural context when they blame Nehru for not adopting the post-1991 economic strategy after Independence. If the post-1991 strategy had been adopted in the 1950s, India would surely have become a 'banana republic'. Conversely, it would not make any sense to have the 1950s economic strategy in the 1990s, when the nature of the global economy, including the Indian economy, had undergone fundamental changes.[21]

The Nehruvian era *created the conditions* for the future 'opening up' and growth by 'un-structuring' many aspects of the inherited colonial structure. Other post-colonial countries too required this period of thirty to forty years of un-structuring before opening up. China needed to go through the Maoist phase before Deng's opening up in the late 1970s could be possible. Today's India is possible *because* of the base laid by the Nehruvian consensus in the early decades after Independence; it has not emerged *despite* it.

Agricultural Transformation

Another canard spread about Nehru is his supposed neglect of agriculture while focusing on industrial development. Nehru was too sophisticated a thinker not to be acutely aware of the complementarity of agricultural and industrial growth. Also, India's food security was an area of great concern because the maintenance of India's sovereignty and ability to stay non-aligned and the welfare of the vast masses of India was involved. Indian agriculture had stagnated and even declined under colonial rule. Per capita agricultural output actually *fell* at the rate of 0.72 per cent per year during 1911–41. Per capita food grains output fell even more sharply by 1.14 per cent per year, a 29 per cent fall over the period.[22] No wonder then that at Independence India was faced with acute food shortage and famine conditions in many areas. Fourteen million tonnes of food had to be imported between 1946 and 1953. There could be no sovereignty if India was dependent on food aid for its very survival. Indian agriculture needed to be revolutionized and Nehru took up the task on a war footing. As Nehru clearly stated in parliament on 15 December 1952:

'We certainly attach importance to industry, but in the present context we attach *far greater importance to agriculture* and food and matters pertaining to agriculture. If our agricultural foundation is not strong then the industry we seek to build will not have a strong basis either. Apart from that, the situation in the country today is such that if our food front cracks up, everything else will crack up too. Therefore we dare not weaken our food front. If our agriculture becomes strongly entrenched, as we hope it will, then it will be relatively easy for us to progress more rapidly on the industrial front, whereas if we concentrate only on industrial development and leave agriculture in a weak condition we shall ultimately be weakening industry. That is why primary attention has been given to agriculture and food and that, I think, is essential in a country like India at the present moment.'[23]

Nehru pushed through the extremely difficult task of land reforms in India *within a democratic framework*, basing himself on the long and powerful heritage of the national and peasant movements. A remarkable achievement in contrast to the *forced* land reforms achieved in Soviet Union and China, costing millions of lives, or the land reforms of Japan under an army of occupation. In 1952, he declared to his party:

'To this task of bringing about *peacefully and cooperatively* essential changes in the *social and economic structure* of the country, the Congress must now address itself with all its strength . . . While the nation must advance on all fronts, the immediate task is to complete the *abolition of zamindari*, jagirdari . . . like systems of land tenure, and thus further the agrarian revolution in India.'[24]

By 1957, the back of the over 150-year-old Zamindari system was broken. Cooperative and institutional credit considerably weakened the stranglehold of the moneylender. Loans advanced by such institutions increased by more than fifteen times, rising from Rs 0.23 billion (Rs 23 crore) in 1950–51 to Rs 3.65 billion (Rs 365 crore) in 1965–66. Such institutional reforms were combined with major investments in scientific agricultural research, irrigation and electric power projects.[25]

Nehru made no false dichotomy between agriculture and industry. Keenly aware that an agrarian transformation was not possible without an industrial and infrastructural transformation, i.e., without electricity, tractors, pumps, chemical fertilizers, etc., he pushed for industrial transformation simultaneously with the agricultural reforms. Electricity generation, for example, increased by over 1300 per cent under his guidance between 1950 and 1965.[26]

The combination of institutional changes (land reforms) and massive state sponsored technological change transformed Indian agriculture rapidly. During the first three plans (leaving out 1965–66, a drought year), Indian agriculture grew at an annual rate of over 3 per cent, a growth rate more than *eight times* the annual growth rate of 0.37 per cent achieved during the half century (1891–1946) of the last phase of colonialism in India.[27]

Attempts are sometimes made to contrast Nehru with his successor Lal Bahadur Shastri, the latter in his all too brief tenure being credited with the ushering in of the Green Revolution strategy. The reality is somewhat different. It was clear that by the late fifties and early sixties, as the benefits from the land reforms that could be carried out in Indian conditions had begun to peak and the possibilities of agricultural growth based on extension of agriculture, i.e., bringing more area into cultivation, were also reaching their limit. Nehru's focus, therefore, inevitably shifted further towards technological solutions. Even the New Agricultural Strategy, associated with the Green Revolution, of picking out select areas with certain natural advantages for intensive development with a package programme (the IADP or the Intensive Agricultural Districts Programme) was launched in fifteen districts, one for each state, on an experimental basis during the Third Plan in Nehru's lifetime—a practice which was to be generalized on a large scale a few years later. As one of the major scholars of the Green Revolution, G.S. Bhalla, put it:

'The qualitative technological transformation in India—the Green Revolution . . . came about not during his lifetime but soon after his death. But the *foundations* for the technological development were laid during Nehru's time.'[28]

Nehru thus not only brought about major institutional reforms (land reforms) in Indian agriculture, he also laid the foundations for the technological reforms, the basis of the 'Green Revolution', which made India food surplus in a remarkably short period.[29] No wonder, Daniel Thorner, one of the keenest observers of Indian agriculture since Independence, noted:

'It is sometimes said that the (initial) five-year plans neglected agriculture. This charge cannot be taken seriously. The facts are that in India's first twenty-one years of Independence more has been done to foster change in agriculture and more change has actually taken place than in the preceding two hundred years.'[30]

Anticipating the Knowledge Revolution

Jawaharlal Nehru saw a focus on scientific education at the highest level as a necessary part of achieving and maintaining sovereignty by reducing dependence on the advanced world. He was acutely aware of India's backwardness in science and technology, an area deliberately left barren in the colonial period, and therefore made massive efforts to overcome this shortcoming. There was an unprecedented increase in the educational opportunities available in science and technology in the universities and institutes set up in the early years after Independence. Almost all the major institutions in this area such as the Indian Institutes of Technology, Indian Institutes of Management, the Council of Scientific and Industrial Research, the Atomic Energy Commission, the Bhabha Atomic Research Centre (with the first atomic reactor going critical in 1956 and the first rocket being tested from Thumba in 1963!), the Indian National Committee for Space Research (the predecessor of the Indian Space Research Organisation, ISRO), the National Physical Laboratory, the National Chemical Laboratory, National Metallurgical Laboratory, the All India Institute of Medical Sciences, the National Institute of Virology, the Defence Research and Development Organisation and numerous other such institutions were all set up in the Nehruvian era. (One must mention here that for Nehru cultivating 'knowledge' was not to be limited to the scientific area. In the 1950s, under his initiative, the Sahitya Akademi, Sangeet Natak Akademi, National School of Drama, Lalit Kala Akademi and the National Council for Applied Economic Research, and the Indian Statistical Institute, were set up, as was the Film and Television Institute of India, in 1960 and the National Institute of Design and the National Council of Educational Research and Training, in 1961).

National expenditure on scientific research and development kept growing rapidly with each plan. For example, it increased from Rs 10 million (Rs 1 crore) in 1949 to Rs 4.5 billion (Rs 450 crore) in 1977. Roughly over the same period, the stock of India's scientific and technical manpower increased more than twelve times from 1,90,000 (1.9 lakh) to 2.32 million (23.2 lakh). A spectacular growth by any standards, a growth whose benefits India reaps today as the world moved towards a 'knowledge' society, a move which Nehru anticipated.[31] It is because Nehru anticipated the knowledge revolution that today India is able to participate in this global phenomenon and nearly half of India's GDP is generated from the service sector, a significant part of which is based on the knowledge revolution. It is not despite Nehru but because of his far-sightedness that India has reached where it has.

One may add that the focus on scientific education at the higher level was not counterpoised to primary education as is often alleged. Nehru's commitment to primary education remained steadfast, from the days of the 1931 Karachi Resolution drafted by him, which committed the state to providing free and compulsory basic education. The government system of primary school education during the Nehruvian era, insufficient though it was, is in stark contrast to the near destruction of that system in today's India where even the poor are increasingly forced to access whatever little education they are able to from the rapacious private sector. Enrolment in schools increased from 23.5 million (2.35 crore) in 1950–51 to 67.7 million (6.77 crore) in 1965–66, a significant increase of 188.1 per cent. (While the increase in admissions at the degree level for engineering and technology increased by 502.4 per cent in the same period, the huge difference is explained partly by the fact of the low base from which it started in 1950–51, only 4100 admissions, increasing to

24,700 in 1965–66, and partly because the need to catch up in this area was critical for maintaining a sovereign, independent path of economic development.)[32] Rather than building on the public education system painstakingly built up in the Nehruvian era at the school level, as well as, at the highest level, it is either being allowed to die, or active efforts are made to dismantle it. The National Education Policy of 2020, which is now being pushed, is a good example of this dismantling, with the state increasingly withdrawing its role in education and handing over this sector to the private sector and even more ominously to foreign universities. Education and health are no longer treated as public goods to be promoted by the state; instead, they are being treated as extremely lucrative areas of private profit. The vast masses of the poor are increasingly denied access to either.

Keeping the Focus on the Poor

Nehru's success in keeping India on the democratic, civil libertarian path against considerable odds (while most other post-colonial countries faltered on this count), by itself ensured that the poor were not altogether left out of the development process and that their condition was not totally ignored. It is now well recognized that democracy is critical for the survival of the poor. It is democracy in India which has ensured that an inflationary path to growth, which hits the poor the hardest, was never adopted. The trend rate of inflation in India since Independence had not touched two digits for several decades.[1] Until 1963, it did not exceed 2 per cent per annum. No government in India irrespective of their political ideology has been able to ignore the political implications of uncontrolled inflation.

Also, it was democracy and civil liberty that ensured that no large-scale famine deaths occurred in India since Independence, despite some extreme conditions created by climatic shocks, while more than 40 million died in famines in China in the late 1950s and '60s, which the world got to know decades later because of the absence of a free media. Amartya Sen has repeatedly emphasized the role of civil liberty and a free press in preventing such mass man-made disasters. With over 100,000 registered newspapers and periodicals and nearly a 1000 satellite channels, dozens of newspapers having a daily readership of more than a million, it is not easy to keep famine conditions under cover in India, despite the mainstream media today functioning as the promoters of government propaganda.

While political democracy was understood by Nehru to be a necessary condition for people's empowerment, it was by no means taken to be sufficient. As he put it in 1952:

'If poverty and low standards continue then democracy, for all its fine institutions and ideals, ceases to be a liberating force. It must therefore aim continuously at the eradication of poverty . . . In other words, *political democracy is not enough*. It must develop into economic democracy also.'[2]

Nehru was deeply aware that active efforts had to be made and institutional structures created which would enable the masses of people to live a life of dignity. He set up the massive Community Development Programme in 1952, aimed at ameliorating all aspects of people's lives in the remote villages, from improvement in agricultural methods to communications, education and health. His basic objective through this programme was 'to unleash forces from below among our people' by creating conditions in which spontaneous growth from below was possible. The ultimate aim was 'progressively producing a measure of equality in opportunity and other things.'[3] A veritable army of Village Level Workers (Gram Sewaks) and Block Development Officers was spread out in the countryside to achieve this goal. As a tendency towards bureaucratization began to emerge in this programme, Nehru tried to integrate it with the Panchayati Raj institutions (elected local self-governing bodies) and set up a large programme of cooperatives in banking, marketing and other services to benefit and empower millions of peasants.[4] Emphasizing the critical role of local village level self-governing cooperative institutions, Nehru said:

'I feel more and more that we must function more from below than from the top. The top is important of course and in the modern world a large measure of centralization is inevitable. Yet *too much centralization means decay at the roots and ultimately a withering of the branches and leaves and flowers.* Therefore we have to encourage these basic organs in the village.'[5]

However, the struggle to make these local institutions function in favour of the most deprived was not an easy one in a society greatly divided by class, caste and gender. In fact, decades after Nehru passed away, Rajiv Gandhi took the initiative to reinvigorate the Panchayati Raj by proposing that elections to these bodies be made *mandatory* and that the deprived castes, tribes *and women* be given adequate representation in them. This resulted in the 73rd and 74th amendments to the Indian Constitution in 1993. The process of trying to empower the poor and disadvantaged is still carrying on as it must in the future, but the foundation was laid by Jawaharlal Nehru.

Nehru was deeply influenced by Marxism since the late 1920s. His contribution in embedding and then making *widely acceptable* the socialist ideal of empowering the poor among the Indian people was immense. Hiren Mukherjee, the legendary parliamentarian and eminent communist leader said about Nehru: 'it was he, largely, who put socialism, so to speak, on India's political map'.[6] The fact that not only the Communists and Socialists but an overwhelming majority of nationalist opinion in India, since the late 1930s, accepted socialism as an objective was, to a great extent, because of Nehru. So deeply did this idea get rooted among the Indian people as a whole that as late as 1980, when the decidedly right-wing Jana Sangh, which was ideologically far from socialism or the national movement, and whose predecessors, the Hindu Mahasabha, and heroes, like Savarkar, were accused of the assassination of Mahatma Gandhi,[7] was reborn in its new avatar as the Bharatiya Janata Party (BJP), it chose to declare its creed as '*Gandhian Socialism*'!

Nehru was able to give the socialist ideal such wide acceptability in India, partly because he made a very early break from a narrow, sectarian and rigid interpretation of Marxism which, Bipan Chandra, India's leading historian of the modern and contemporary period, called 'Stalin–Marxism'.[8] Nehru was among the first in the world to make this break from Stalin–Marxism. Roughly at the same time as the famous Italian Marxist Antonio Gramsci (with whom comparisons have already been made at the beginning of this work), Nehru, in the late 1930s, was groping for a strategy of social transformation in a democratic or semi-democratic framework, which was different from the insurrectionary and violent Bolshevik model that was not suitable for such situations. Nehru was fortunate in being witness to, and part of, the Gandhian struggle for freedom which was till then, and perhaps remains till today, 'the only actual historical example of a semi-democratic or democratic-type state structure being replaced or transformed, of the broadly Gramscian theoretical perspective of a war of position being successfully practised.' The fact that Gramsci saw this 'as the only possible strategy' for social transformation 'in the developed countries of the west' underlines the huge significance of the Gandhian movement to the world as a whole.[9]

Learning from the practice of the Gandhian movement made it easier for Nehru to break from the Stalin–Marxist paradigm and argue somewhat precociously that, while there could be no true democracy without socialism, there could be no socialism without democracy. He insisted that civil liberty and democracy had to be basic parts of socialism. The socialist transformation required *societal consensus*, the consent of the overwhelming majority of the people. It could not be a minority revolution, led by a band of highly committed revolutionaries, a 'dictatorship of the proletariat'. It was also not enough just to have a majority. To succeed, it had to be a socialism acceptable to all sections, by an *overwhelming majority*. Nehru was anticipating what later events were to validate and what was to be slowly accepted globally by increasing sections of the Left. He made this shift long before this change was acceptable to any significant trend in the communist movement in India and the world. The emergence of Eurocommunism, which made similar assumptions, occurred only in the 1970s, and '80s. Nehru's shift was, therefore, for very long analysed by the orthodox Left as the 'diluting' of his commitment to socialism for various reasons such as pragmatic pressures, the influence of Gandhiji or even his alleged desire to be in power.

By the late 1930s, Nehru began to veer towards the position that Socialism could not be brought about by coercion or force. How can you arrive at a consensus by force? He argued that to achieve the desirable end of socialist transformation, one should not adopt the means of hatred and violence, and that a socialistic pattern of society could be achieved through non-violent and peaceful means. Fully in tune with the Gandhian notion that wrong means could not achieve the right ends, he declared:

> 'There is always a close and intimate relationship between the end we aim at and the means adopted to attain it. Even if the end is right and the means are wrong, it will vitiate the end or divert us in a wrong direction.'[10]

Also, arriving at a socialist consensus would mean that one would have to view it as a process, and not an event arrived at in a 'revolutionary moment.' This would have to be a long drawn out process with its ups and downs, a process which may have to at times slow down, moderate or tone down its immediate goals, in order to carry the bulk of the people along, including those who held opposing positions. Nehru, writing from prison in the 1940s, and describing his understanding of how the National Planning Committee, set up by the Congress in 1938, should move in a socialist direction, argued:

> '. . . this was to be attempted in the context of *democratic freedom* and with a large measure of

cooperation of some at least of the groups who were normally opposed to the socialist doctrine. That cooperation seemed to me worthwhile *even if it involved toning down* or weakening of the plan in some respects.'[11]

Nehru was to retain throughout his life this nuanced persuasive style of functioning while remaining resolute in his goals, which brought him the support, love and admiration of the millions in a manner which was surpassed only by Gandhiji. As a true disciple of the master, while appealing to all sections of society, he succeeded in keeping his gaze focused on the poor, the oppressed and the disadvantaged. His great achievement was that he got a very large part of Indian society, individuals and institutions, to share his socialist vision. In the Nehruvian period, from the planning commission and the public sector bureaucracy to the media and popular films, the socialist objective was seen as a desirable one, not defined in any narrow, fundamentalist way, but as Nehru broadly outlined it.

The land reforms, the Green Revolution, the Community Development Programme, the emergence of the public sector, the focus on education and health being a public responsibility, protecting of working class rights and the popularizing of the socialist ideal were giant steps taken by Nehru that greatly contributed to an equitable society. Many of these steps are being reversed today with the privatization of public sector enterprises and, more shockingly, with the handing over of the education and health departments to the rapacious private sector, rapid informalization of labour with no trade union rights and making a mockery of the socialist ideal. The results are there for the world to see. India is witnessing obscene levels of inequality where we boast of our large number of billionaires while nearly half our children are malnourished. The world was shocked by the images of floating dead bodies in the river Ganga, victims of the corona virus epidemic, as the relatives of the deceased were too poor to do the last rites of their dear ones, or those of thousands of migrant workers walking hundreds of miles to their villages at temperatures of 45 degrees centigrade, dragging their old and infirm and children to avoid starvation because of the sudden lockdown without adequate state support. We are slipping rapidly in the human development index and are shamefully ranked 111 out of 125 countries today in the Global Hunger Index, below many sub-

Saharan African countries and much below every other South Asian country, with Sri Lanka at sixty, Nepal at sixty-nine and Bangladesh at eighty-one![12]

Sixty years after his death, with infinitely higher economic capacity to empower the poor, when we falter miserably on this count, we realize how important it is to remember Nehru's legacy.

Scientific Temper

Nehru's focus on the need to develop a 'scientific temper', a term he coined in his *Discovery of India*, which the Constitution of India reiterated in article 51A, laying down the fundamental duties of every citizen of India, is being made a mockery of today. Nehru said:

'The scientific temper points out the way along which man should travel . . . It is the scientific approach, the adventurous and yet critical temper of science, the search for truth and new knowledge, the refusal to accept anything without testing and trial, the capacity to change previous conclusions in the face of evidence, the reliance on the observed fact and not pre-conceived theory, the hard discipline of the mind—all this is necessary, not merely for the application of science but for life itself and the solution of its many problems.'[1]

Nehru tried to imbibe this spirit in his thinking and action throughout his life.

What a contrast today! The *Guardian* quoted the current prime minister mixing up mythology about gods and goddesses with history and science, while inaugurating a new modern hospital in Mumbai:

> 'We can feel proud of what our country achieved in medical science at one point of time,' the prime minister told a gathering of doctors and other professionals at a hospital in Mumbai . . . 'We all read about Karna in the Mahabharata. If we think a little more, we realise that the Mahabharata says Karna was not born from his mother's womb. This means that genetic science was present at that time. That is why Karna could be born outside his mother's womb . . . We worship Lord Ganesha. There must have been some plastic surgeon at that time who got an elephant's head on the body of a human being and began the practice of plastic surgery.'[2]

The *Hindustan Times* reported that the governor of Bengal, committing violence on both science and history, said, while addressing a science and engineering fair in Kolkata that the 'mythological character Arjuna's arrows had nuclear power and chariots mentioned in the Mahabharata actually flew.'[3] He has since been promoted to the post of the vice president of India. The erstwhile RSS chief (*sarsangchalak*) K.S. Sudarshan, an engineer by training, reportedly talked about how sage Bharadwaja and Raja Bhoj, in times gone by, not only 'described the construction of aeroplanes' but discussed 'details like what types of aeroplanes would fly at what height, what kind of problems they might encounter, how to overcome those problems, etc.'[4]

No wonder that the corona virus was being fought with gobar (cow dung), gomutra (cow urine), thali (metal plate) banging, tali (clapping), shining mobile phone torches, Ganga-snan (dip in the Ganges) and unverified medicines made by a much-favoured yogi![5] The Supreme Court had to intervene to call a halt to such false claims made by the yogi.[6]

* * *

In sum, it is as if the political leaders have *reversed* their roles. From that of pulling up society and bringing it in line with the highest global civilizational values, a role performed by the leaders of the Indian national movement like Gandhiji and Nehru, to that of pushing society back by appealing to sectarian identities, acquisitive instincts and traditional prejudices. The hegemonic 'Idea of India', the 'common sense' of the Indian people, created by the Indian national movement, is severely challenged today. That challenge is not coming from a 'backward', 'traditional' people but from their leaders and the state machinery.

Nehru's fantastic effort to raise India from what Tagore called the 'mud and filth' left behind by the British has now been replaced with the Indian people being pushed back into that same 'mud and filth' of ignorance, obscurantism, disempowerment, unfreedom and, above all, communal hatred.

Notes

Demonizing Nehru

1. See Aditya Mukherjee and Mridula Mukherjee, 'Weaponising History: The Hindutva Communal Project' *The Wire,* 10 April 2023, https://m. thewire.in/article/history/weaponising-history-the-hindu-communal-project; Mridula Mukherjee, 'History Wars: The Case of Gandhi-Nehru-Patel', in IIC Quarterly, Volume 49, Summer 2022, Number 1, pp. 39–41. See also Aditya Mukherjee, Mridula Mukherjee and Sucheta Mahajan, *RSS, School Texts and the Murder of Mahatma Gandhi: The Hindu Communal Project,* Sage, New Delhi, 2008, an enlarged, revised edition, to be shortly published by Penguin Random House India.

2 B. Gopal Krishnan in 'Kesari', Rashtriya Swayamsevak Sangh (RSS) mouthpiece in Kerala,

17 October 2014, see https://indianexpress.com/
article/india/india-others/godse-should-have-
targeted-nehru-says-rss-mouthpiece/ accessed on 17
August 2021 and *Hindustan Times*, 25 October 2014,
https://www.hindustantimes.com/india/godse-
should-have-killed-nehru-says-kesari-edit/story-
AZsX4GpYNgQi76e6F4Dv8M.html accessed on
23 August 2024.

3   N.V. Ravindranathan Nair in *The New Indian
Express*, 26 October 2014, see https://www.new
indianexpress.com/states/kerala/2014/Oct/26/rss-
disassociates-itself-from-kesari-article-675369.html
accessed on 16 July 2024

4   *The Times of India*, 8 May 2016, https://timesofindia.
indiatimes.com/india/references-to-jawaharlal-
nehru-dropped-in-new-rajasthan-school-textbook-
congress-cries-foul/articleshow/52177280.cms,
The Indian Express, 26 May 2016, https://indian
express.com/article/india/india-news-india/
jawaharlal-nehru-erased-from-rajasthan-school-
textbook-2789754/ accessed on 4 November 2023.

5   See for example, *The Times of India*, 30 August 2021,
https://timesofindia.indiatimes.com/india/other-
posters-will-have-nehrus-image-unnecessary-

controversy-over-issue-ichr-official/articleshow/
85735778.cms, accessed on 3 November 2023. *The Hindu,* 29 August 2021, https://www.thehindu.
com/news/national/chidambaram-slams-ichr-for-
omitting-nehrus-photo-from-poster-celebrating-
indias-Independence/article36161501.ece, accessed
on 3 November 2023.

6   For a detailed discussion on Savarkar's apology
and his role after his release, see Aditya Mukherjee,
et al., *RSS, School Texts and the Murder of Mahatma*
Gandhi, (New Delhi, Sage, 2008). Also see, f.n. 48 in
Nehru On Communal Challenge and f.n. 7 in Focus
on Poor below.

7   For a detailed discussion on the close link between
colonialism and communalism, see chapter 10,
'Colonialism and Communalism: A Legacy Haunting
India Today', in Aditya Mukherjee, *Political
Economy of Colonial and Post-Colonial India'* (Delhi:
Primus Books, 2022).

Nehru and the Discipline of History

1   'Jawaharlal Nehru's Historical Vision' in Irfan Habib,
The National Movement: Studies in Ideology and

History (New Delhi: Tulika Books, 2013) p. 38–39, emphasis mine. See, for a similar appreciation of Nehru as Habib's, Joachim Heidrich, 'Jawaharlal Nehru's Perception of History', (Mimeo.) in a fascinating Seminar on 'Jawaharlal Nehru as Writer and Historian', in which a large number of scholars from all over the world participated, organized by the Jawaharlal Nehru Memorial Fund and Jawaharlal Nehru Memorial Museum and Library, New Delhi, 23–26 October 1989.

2   'On Understanding History', Inaugural address at the silver jubilee session of the Indian Historical Records Commission, 23 December 1948, *Jawaharlal Nehru's Speeches*, Vol. 1 (1946–49) (New Delhi: Publications Division, Government of India, 4th edition, 1983), pp. 354, 357–58.

3   Habib, Jawaharlal Nehru's *Historical Vision,* p. 40.

4   'On Understanding History', 1948, p. 358.

5   The discussion on the Somanatha and the quotation from K.M. Munshi is from Romila Thapar, 'Perspectives of the History of Somanatha', Umashankar Joshi Memorial Lecture, 29 December 2012, and *Somanatha: The Many Voices of a History* (New Delhi: Penguin, 2003).

6 Jawaharlal Nehru, *The Discovery of India* (first published The Signet Press, Calcutta, 1946), (Gurgaon: Penguin Random House India, 2010), pp. 250–54. All references to *Discovery* are from this later edition.

7 'The Function of Universities', address to a special convocation of the University of Allahabad, 13 December 1947, *Jawaharlal Nehru's Speeches*, Vol. 1, pp. 331–32.

8 See for example, Amartya Sen, *The Idea of Justice* (London: Penguin), 2009, Ch.15, pp. 321–25; Amartya Sen, *The Argumentative Indian: Writings on Indian History, Culture and Identity,* (London: Penguin, 2005), and Amartya Sen 'History and the Enterprise of Knowledge' address delivered at the Indian History Congress, Calcutta, January 2001.

9 *Discovery,* p. 263. A song written and composed by Khusrau: '*Chaap Tilak Sab Chheeni re Mose Naina Milaike*', for example, is sung till today by millions across religions in the Indian subcontinent, including Pakistan and Bangladesh, till today.

10 *Discovery,* p. 51.

11 *Discovery,* p. 254 and 'Importance of Archaeological Study', Speech delivered at the Centenary celebrations

of the Archaeological Survey of India and the International Conference of Asian Archaeology, New Delhi, 14 December 1961, *Jawaharlal Nehru's Speeches,* Vol. 4, 1957–63, (New Delhi: Publications Division, Government of India, 1964), pp. 179–81. Emphasis mine.

12 *Discovery,* p. 258.

13 See, for example, Romila Thapar, Harbans Mukhia and Bipan Chandra, *Communalism and the Writing of Indian History* (Delhi: People's Publishing House, 1969) and Micheguglielmo Torri, 'For a New Periodization of Indian History: The History of India as Part of the History of the World', *Studies in History,* Vol. 30, Issue 1, 12 May 2014.

14 'On Understanding History', 1948, pp. 353–54.

15 Ibid. pp. 354–55. Emphasis mine.

16 See chapter 13, 'Challenges to the Social Sciences in the Twenty-First Century: Perspectives from the Global South' in Aditya Mukherjee, *Political Economy of Colonial and Post-Colonial India'* (Delhi: Primus Books, 2022), for a discussion on Eurocentric/colonial perspectives continuing to be a challenge in the third world and even among

the finest historians of the West, including Marxist historians.

17 'A New Perspective of History', Inaugural Address to the Asian History Congress, New Delhi, 9 December 1961, *Jawaharlal Nehru's Speeches,* Vol. 4, 1957–63, p. 179.

18 'A New Perspective of History', 1961, p. 178.

19 'On the Understanding of History', Foreword to a book, 8 October 1933, *Selected Works of Jawaharlal Nehru,* (hereafter *SWJN*), 1st *Series,* Volume 6, 1979, New Delhi, pp.199–200.

20 'A New Perspective of History', 1961, p. 178.

21 For a recent example of this obfuscation see, 'Empire and Transformation: The Politics of Difference', Keynote Lecture by Jane Burbank, New York University, at the 6th International Symposium of Comparative Research on Major Regional Powers in Eurasia Comparing Modern Empires: Imperial Rule and Decolonization in the Changing World Order, Hokkaido University, Japan, 20 January 2012, and for the development of her argument with sources and citations Jane Burbank and Frederick Cooper, *Empire in World History: Power and Politics of*

Difference (Princeton, New Jersey: Princeton University Press, 2010).

22 'On the Understanding of History', 1933, p. 200.

23 *The Wire,* 19 July 2023, https://thewire.in/history/ claiming-india-saw-1000-years-of-foreign-rule-trivialises-british-colonial-exploitation accessed on 5 November 2023, *The Wire,* 15 August 2023, https:// thewire.in/government/Independence-day-modi-speech-slavery-manipur, accessed on 24 August 2023. The PM made the same statement addressing a joint session of the US Congress on 22 June 2023, https://scroll.in/latest/1051436/india-got-freedom-after-1000-years-of-foreign-rule-says-narendra-modi-at-us-congress, accessed on 24 August 2023. He talked of 1200 years of slavery in his Motion of Thanks to the President's address to the joint session of the Parliament on 9 June 2014. https://www. firstpost.com/politics/1200-years-of-servitude-pm-modi-offers-food-for-thought-1567805.html,   13 June 2014, accessed on 24 August 2023.

24 *Discovery,* pp. 254–55. Emphasis mine.

25 *A New Perspective of History,* 1961, p. 178.

26 'On the Understanding of History', 1933, p. 199. Emphasis mine.

27 'On Understanding History', 1948, p. 354. Emphasis mine.

28 'On Understanding History', 1948, pp. 354, 356–57. Emphasis mine.

29 Ibid. pp.355–56.

30 'On the Understanding of History', 1933, p. 200.

31 For example, R.S. Sharma, Romila Thapar, Bipan Chandra, Satish Chandra, Irfan Habib, D.N. Jha, Arjun Dev, Shireen Moosvi, Ranabir Chakroborty, Upinder Singh and others.

32 Bipan Chandra outlines the critical shift in Nehru's thinking and the impact of Gandhiji. He was among the first in the Left to see this shift positively. See his seminal essay, 'Jawaharlal Nehru in Historical Perspective' in *Writings of Bipan Chandra: The Making of Modern India: From Marx to Gandhi* (New Delhi: Orient Blackswan, 2012). For a brief summary, see my Introduction to the above volume reproduced in Aditya Mukherjee, *Political Economy of Colonial and Post-colonial India* (Delhi: Primus Books, 2022).

33 See Bipan Chandra, 'Jawaharlal Nehru in Historical Perspective', pp. 113–14.

34 Quoted in Manash Firaq Bhattacharjee, *Nehru and the Spirit of India* (Gurgaon: Viking, 2022) p. 181.

35 Perry Anderson, *The Indian Ideology* (Gurgaon: Three Essays Collective, 2012), pp. 52–53.

36 Bhattacharjee, *Nehru and the Spirit of India*, p. 21.

37 Bipan Chandra, 'Jawaharlal Nehru in Historical Perspective', p. 150–51.

38 See Tadd Graham Fernée, 'The Gandhian Circle of Moral Consideration', *Social Scientist,* Vol. 50, No. 11–12 November–December 2022, where he quotes Gandhi, comparing the French and Russian Revolution with the Indian struggle.

39 Tadd Graham Fernée, *Enlightenment and Violence: Modernity and Nation Making,* Sage Series in Modern Indian History (New Delhi: Sage, 2014), and Tadd Graham Fernée, *Beyond the Circle of Violence and Progress: Ethics and Material Development in India and Egypt, Anti-colonial Struggle to Independence* (Shimla: Indian Institute of Advanced Study, 2023).

40 Bhattacharjee, *Nehru and the Spirit of India,* pp. 16, 18, 181.

Nehru and the Idea of India

1 *Collected Works of Mahatma Gandhi*, Vol. 76 (New Delhi: Publications Division, 1958-84), p. 389–90. The imagery used by Gandhiji for futile attempts to divide is very applicable to the current effort by the communal forces to constantly try to denigrate our freedom struggle by trying to point out differences between our national heroes like Gandhi, Nehru, Patel, Bose, Bhagat Singh, etc.

2 Quoted in Bipan Chandra, Mridula Mukherjee, Aditya Mukherjee, *India Since Independence* (New Delhi: Penguin Books India, 2008), p. 23.

3 For an analysis of the colonial situation before Independence and the structural break made after Independence under Nehru's guidance, see Aditya Mukherjee, 'Return of the Colonial in Indian Economic History: The Last Phase of Colonialism in India,' Presidential Address, 68th session of the Indian History Congress, (Modern India), 2007, reproduced as Chapter 1 in Aditya Mukherjee, *Political Economy of Colonial and Post-Colonial India* (Delhi: Primus Books, 2022).

4   For a brief overview of Nehru's outstanding contribution in the sphere of foreign policy and international relations, and a reasoned explanation on issues relating to Kashmir, Pakistan and China for which he has been much reviled, see, Mridula Mukherjee, 'Foreign Policy: The Nehru Era' in Bipan Chandra, Mridula Mukherjee and Aditya Mukherjee, *India Since Independence* (New Delhi: Penguin Books India, 2008). The above quotation is from this work. Emphasis mine. See also, V.P. Dutt, *India's Foreign Policy* (New Delhi: Vikas, 1984), B.R. Nanda ed., *Indian Foreign Policy: The Nehru Years* (Delhi: Vikas, 1976) and a very important collection of Nehru's speeches and statements on foreign policy between September 1946 and April 1961 in, Jawaharlal Nehru, *India's Foreign Policy*, (New Delhi, Publications Division, 1961).

Nehru on the Communal Challenge

1   See Mridula Mukherjee, 'Jawaharlal Nehru's Finest Hour: The Struggle for a Secular India', *Studies in People's History,* Vol. 1, No. 2, 2014, https://journals.sagepub.com/doiabs/10.1177/

2348448914549900?journal Code=sipa and Mridula Mukherjee, 'Communal Threat and Secular Resistance: From Noakhali to Gujarat', *Presidential Address (Modern India), Indian History Congress,* Malda, February 2011, for a detailed discussion on how the Indian nationalists, led by Nehru and Gandhiji, met the communal challenge in this period. This section relies heavily on the above two works. See also, Sucheta Mahajan, *Independence and Partition: The Erosion of Colonial Power in India* (New Delhi: Sage, 2000), and Rakesh Batabyal, *Communalism in Bengal: From Famine to Noakhali* (New Delhi: Sage, 2005).

2 Mridula Mukherjee, 'Jawaharlal Nehru's Finest Hour . . .'

3 Speech at Biharsharif, 4 November 1946, *SWJN,* 2nd Series, Vol.1, New Delhi, 1984, p. 57.

4 *SWJN,* 2nd Series, Vol. 4, p. 2.

5 *SWJN,* 2nd Series, Vol. 4, p. 9.

6 *Jawaharlal Nehru: Letters to Chief Ministers* (hereafter *LCM,*) 5 February 1948, Vol. 1 (New Delhi: Jawaharlal Nehru Memorial Fund and Oxford University Press, 1985), p. 56.

7 Ibid. p. 57.

8   *LCM,* 20 July 1949 and 1 August 1949, Vol. 1, pp. 412–13, 428.

9   Mridula Mukherjee, see f.n. 1 and f.n. 2 above.

10 See Soutik Biswas, 'Invisible in our own country: Being Muslim in Modi's India'. https://www.bbc.com/news/world-asia-india-68498675 accessed on 18 July 2024, for an account of how abandoning secularism is undermining Indian democracy.

11 Jawaharlal Nehru, *An Autobiography* (New Delhi: Oxford University Press, 1980), first published in 1936, pp. 458–72. The quote in the previous sentence is from p. 60.

12 Statement to the Press, 5 January 1934, *SWJN,* 1st Series, Vol. 6, 1974, p. 182.

13 For example, W.C. Smith, *Modern Islam in India: A Social Analysis* (London: Victor Gollancz, 1946), Francis Robinson, *Separatism Among Indian Muslims: The Politics of the United Provinces' Muslims, 1860–1923* (Cambridge: Cambridge University Press, 1974) and a classic, comprehensive analytical work on the subject by Bipan Chandra, *Communalism in Modern India* (New Delhi: Vikas, 1984) (New Delhi: Har-Anand, 3rd revised edition, 2008).

14 *Autobiography,* p. 460.

15 *Autobiography,* pp. 460–67.

16 *The Statesman,*17 January 1952, quoted in N.L. Gupta, ed., *Nehru on Communalism* (New Delhi: Sampradayikta Virodhi Committee, 1965), p. 239. Emphasis mine.

17 See Aditya Mukherjee, *Imperialism, Nationalism and the Making of the Indian Capitalist Class: 1920–1947* (New Delhi: Sage, 2002), new edition in Penguin Random House India, forthcoming. See also Aditya Mukherjee, 'Imperialism, Nationalism and the Nation State', Ch. 6 in *Political Economy of Colonial and Post-Colonial India,* for a gradual shift in the capitalist class position after Independence.

18 Nehru's speech in Delhi on 2 October 1951, *SWJN,* 2nd series, Vol. 16, pt. II, pp. 115–16.

19 See, for example, A.K. Bhattacharya and Paranjoy Guha Thakurta, 'Contours of Crony Capitalism in the Modi Raj'. in *Majoritarian State: How Hindu Nationalism is Changing India.* Editors, Angana P. Chatterji, Thomas Blom Hansen and Christophe Jaffrelot (Oxford University Press, 2019) DOI: 10.1093/oso/9780190078171.003.0011, 'Crony capitalism in Modi's India', by Camille Auvray Le

Monde diplomatique – English, https://monde diplo.com/2024/04/04india, 19 April 2024, accessed on 26 July 2024, Frontline 30 March 2024, https://frontline.thehindu.com/columns/2024-general-election-crony-capitalism-authoritarianism-ed-raids-and-arrests/article68006060.ece, accessed on 26 July 2024, and The Wire, 3 May 2024, https://thewire.in/media/how-indian-corporate-giants-have-been-tightening-their-grip-over-the-media accessed on 26 July 2024.

20 *SWJN*, 1st Series, Vol. 6, p. 183.

21 Speech at a public meeting in Hyderabad, 15 December 1951. A.I.R. tapes, Original in Hindi, *SWJN,* 2nd series, Vol. 17, pp. 65–66.

22 *SWJN*, 1st Series, Vol. 6, p. 183.

23 Jawaharlal Nehru, *Recent Writings and Essays,* Allahabad, 1937 extract in N.L. Gupta, ed., *Nehru and Communalism*, p. 26, emphasis mine.

24 *LCM*, 1 August 1949, Vol. 1, p. 428, emphasis mine. See Mridula Mukherjee, 'Jawaharlal Nehru's Finest Hour? The Struggle for a Secular India', *Studies in People's History*, Vol. 1, No. 2, December 2014, and Aditya Mukherjee, 'Inclusive Democracy and

People's Empowerment: The Legacy of Jawaharlal Nehru', *EPW*, Vol. 50, No. 16, 18 April 2015.

25 8 February 1952, *SWJN,* 1995, Vol. 17, 2nd Series, p. 133. Emphasis mine.

26 Ibid. Emphasis mine.

27 Jawaharlal Nehru, 'Hindu and Muslim Communalism', *The Tribune*, 30 November 1933, *SWJN,* Vol. 6, Series 1, p. 171.

28 *SWJN,* 1995, Vol. 17, Series 2, p. 144. Emphasis mine.

29 Nehru's speech on 2 October 1951, 'Relevance of Mahatma Gandhi', *SWJN,* 1994, Vol. 16, Pt. II, pp. 102–19 and as reported in the *Statesman,* 3 October 1951, quoted in N.L. Gupta, 'Nehru and Communalism', pp. 224–28. Emphasis mine.

30 *LCM*, Vol II, p. 213.

31 N.L. Gupta, 'Nehru and Communalism', p. 29–30.

32 *The Statesman*, 19 October 1951, quoted in Ibid., p. 232.

33 *The Statesman,* 24 November 1951, quoted in Ibid. p. 234.

34 4 June 1949, *LCM*, Vol. 1, p. 372. Emphasis mine.

35 *SWJN,* 2005, Vol. 35, 2nd Series, pp. 3–24, particularly pp. 12, 16–17 and 23. Emphasis mine.

36 https://vidyabharti.net/status-work-session-2022-23-glance Vidya Bharati official website accessed on 10 September 2023.

37 Reputed historians like R.S. Sharma, Romila Thapar, Satish Chandra, Bipan Chandra and Arjun Dev wrote textbooks for children from class VI to XII.

38 See, for a description of this process, Aditya Mukherjee, et al., *RSS, School Texts* . . . and Aditya Mukherjee and Mridula Mukherjee, 'Weaponising History: The Hindutva Communal Project', *The Wire,* 10 April 2023, https://m.thewire.in/article/history/weaponising-history-the-hindu-communal-project

39 Irfan Habib, Suvira Jaiswal and Aditya Mukherjee, *History in the New NCERT Textbooks: A Report and Index of Errors,* approved and published by the Executive Committee of the Indian History Congress, Kolkata, 2003.

40 Secular activist and editor of the journal *Communalism Combat,* Teesta Setalvad, has been making this point repeatedly. See also, Ashutosh Varshney, 'Gujarat 2002 was independent India's first full-blooded pogrom. Delhi 1984 was a semi-

pogrom' See https://theprint.in/opinion/gujarat-2002-was-independent-indias-first-full-blooded-pogrom-delhi-1984-was-a-semi-pogrom/371684/ accessed on 18 July 2024.

41 Among those who firmly took positions against the effort to communalize education were the former President of India, K.R. Narayanan, Amartya Sen, Romila Thapar, Satish Chandra, Bipan Chandra, Irfan Habib, Vir Sanghvi and Dileep Padgaonkar. Their positions are quoted in Mridula Mukherjee and Aditya Mukherjee, *Communalisation of Education: The History Textbooks Controversy*, with an introduction by the authors, (Delhi: Delhi Historians' Group, 2002).

42 See the RSS mouthpiece, *Organiser*, 4 November 2001.

43 See *Indian Express*, 20 December 2001, and *Hindustan Times*, 8 December 2001.

44 Aditya Mukherjee, et al., *RSS School Texts*...

45 See Aditya Mukherjee and Mridula Mukherjee, 'Weaponising History: The Hindutva Communal Project' *The Wire*, 10 April 2023, https://m.thewire.in/article/history/weaponising-history-the-hindu-communal-project

46 Nehru's article, 'Hindu and Muslim Communalism', *The Tribune,* 30 November 1933, SWJN, 1974, Vol. 6, 1st Series, pp. 164–65, 168–69. All the quotations in the last three paragraphs are from here. Emphasis mine.

47 *Autobiography,* p. 468.

48 Linlithgow, Viceroy, to Zetland, Secretary of State, 7 October 1939, *Zetland Papers,* Vol. 18, Reel No. 6.

49 *SWJN,* Vol. 6, 1st Series, p. 162–63.

50 *SWJN,* Vol. 6, 1st Series, pp. 165.

51 Ibid. p. 163.

52 See my critique of Perry Anderson in Chapter 13, 'Challenges to the Social Sciences in the Twenty-First Century: Perspectives from the Global South' in Aditya Mukherjee, *Political Economy of Colonial and Post-Colonial India.*

53 All quotations are from the chapter titled 'The Citizen and the Secular State Business' in Bhattacharjee, *Nehru and the Spirit of India,* particularly pp. 86–112, see also pp. 90–91, 96 and 110. For a detailed analysis of Bhattacharjee's book and the similarities with Perry Anderson in a false understanding of the Indian national movement and Nehru, see my review of his book, Aditya Mukherjee, 'A Relook at

Jawaharlal Nehru,' *The Wire*, https://m.thewire.in/article/books/a-relook-at-jawaharlal-nehru

54 This Nehru said at the Banaras Hindu University in the presence of Madan Mohan Malaviya, a leading figure of the Hindu Mahasabha, on 12 November 1933. No pandering to the audience. *SWJN,*1974, Vol. VI, p. 157–58. Emphasis mine.

55 *Autobiography,* p. 467. Emphasis mine.

56 *The Statesman*, 19 October 1951, quoted in N.L. Gupta, *Nehru and Communalism*, p. 229. Emphasis mine.

57 *SWJN,* 1st Series, Vol. 6, pp. 165–66. Emphasis mine.

58 Ibid. p. 162.

59 Even such a fine scholar and critic of Hindu communalism as Christophe Jaffrelot uses the phrase 'Hindu nationalism' routinely. See his books, *The Hindu Nationalist Movement in India,* (New York: Columbia University Press, 1998), or *Hindu Nationalism: A Reader,* (Ranikhet: Permanent Black, 2009).

60 Anderson, *The Indian Ideology.* See also, Chs. 6, 8 and 13 in Aditya Mukherjee, *Political Economy of Colonial and Post-Colonial India,* for an appraisal

of Anderson and other such critiques of Indian nationalism.

61 *Writings of Bipan Chandra,* p. 130. See also Mridula Mukherjee, 'Jawaharlal Nehru's Finest Hour? The Struggle for a Secular India', *Studies in People's History,* Vol. 1, Issue 2, December 2014.

62 *LCM,* 7 December 1947, Vol. 1, p. 10. Emphasis mine.

63 *LCM*, 1 August 1949, Vol. 1, p. 428. Emphasis mine.

64 *The Statesman*, 19 October 1951, quoted in N.L. Gupta, *Nehru and Communalism*, p. 231. See also S. Gopal, *Mainstream*, 12 November 1988, and *Jawaharlal Nehru: A Biography,* Vol. 1 (New Delhi: Oxford University Press, 1975.)

65 Wardha, 13 March 1948, *SWJN*, 1987, 2nd Series, Vol. 5, p. 75.

66 *SWJN,* 2nd Series, Vol. 16, Pt. II, p. 11. Emphasis mine.

67 Prabhat Patnaik, *The Telegraph Online*, 15 August 2022,http://www.telegraphindia.com/india/fascism-arrives-in-camouflage-says-prabhat-patnaik/cid/1880205 accessed on 1 December 2023 and Prabhat Patnaik, 'The Fascism of our Times', *Social Scientist,* Vol. 21, Nos. 3/4, March–April 1993. See

also Chaitanya Krishna, ed., *Fascism in India: Faces, Fangs and Facts* (New Delhi: Manak, 2003).

68 Jason Stanley, *How Fascism Works: The Politics of Us and Them* (New York, Random House, 2018).

69 https://www.theguardian.com/commentis free/2023/sep/08/biden-india-modi-g20-autocrat *The Guardian,* 8 September 2023, accessed on 8 September 2023. Emphasis mine. See also https://scroll.in/article/1055943/arundhati-roy-the-dismantling-of-democracy-in-india-will-affect-the-whole-world where Arundhati Roy, like Stanley, is reminding us that democracy in India is a public good for the whole world which cannot be allowed to wither away.

70 *The Telegraph,* 6 August 2023.

71 The *Indian Express, The Hindu* and The *Times of India,* 8 August 2023. Emphasis mine. Also see, https://www.livelaw.in/top-stories/punjab-haryana-high-court-asks-on-nuh-demolition-drive-whether-buildings-belonging-to-particular-community-brought-down-as-exercise-of-ethnic-cleansing-234623, accessed on 9 August 2023. Emphasis mine.

72 Jullunder, 24 February 1948, *SWJN,* 1987, 2nd Series, Vol. 5, p. 65.

Building Democracy

1 Amartya Sen uses this term as early as 1993 to describe one segment of Hindu communalism, in an article he wrote shortly after the demolition of the Babri Masjid by Hindu communalists. See Amartya Sen, 'The Threats to Secular India', *The New York Review,* 8 April 1993.

2 *Michelguglielmo Torri,* 'India 2020: The Deepening Crisis of Democracy,' *Asia Maior*, Vol. XXXI, 2020.

3 All the citations in this paragraph are from https://www.bbc.com/news/world-asia-india-56393944 and https://timesofindia.indiatimes.com/blogs/toi-edit-page/a-more-nuanced-democracy-there-is-no-need-for-it-to-be-only-what-the-west-says-it-must-be/ accessed on 28 October 2021.

4 See R. Jagannathan, 'A More Nuanced Democracy: There Is No Need for It to Be Only What the West Says It Must Be' https://timesofindia.indiatimes.com/blogs/toi-edit-page/a-more-nuanced-democracy-there-is-no-need-for-it-to-be-only-what-the-west-says-it-must-be/ accessed on 26 August 2024.

5 R. K. Karanjia, *The Philosophy of Mr Nehru,* p. 123, quoted in Bipan Chandra, 'Jawaharlal Nehru in

Historical Perspective', in *The Writings of Bipan Chandra: The Making of Modern India from Marx to Gandhi*, New Delhi, 2012, p. 136. Emphasis mine.

6   *Harijan*, 24 June 1939, *Collected Works of Mahatma Gandhi*, Vol. 69, p. 356.

7   Pranab Mukherjee, Aditya Mukherjee, et al., eds., *Congress and the Making of the Indian Nation*, Vol. II, (New Delhi: Academic Publishers, 2011), p. 19. This volume is a collection of important resolutions, manifestos and speeches relating to the Indian National Congress from 1920 to 2009.

8   Mridula Mukherjee, 'Civil Liberties and Indian Nationalism', in Rohit Azad et al., ed., *What the Nation Really Needs to Know: The JNU Nationalism Lectures* (Noida: Harper Collins, 2016), p. 73.

9   See *SWJN*, 1st Series, Vol. 7, pp. 420–21, 425–28.

10   *SWJN*, 1st Series, Vol. 11, p. 367.

11   R. K. Karanjia, quoted in Bipan Chandra, 'Jawaharlal Nehru in Historical Perspective', see f.n. 5. Emphasis mine.

12   Speech at Trivandrum, 2 June 1950, in *The National Herald*, 3 June 1950, cited in S. Gopal, *Jawaharlal Nehru, A Biography*, Vol. 2, 1947–1956, (New Delhi:

Oxford University Press, 1979), p. 68. Emphasis mine.

13 The article was published in *The Modern Review* of Calcutta in November 1937, under the name of Chanakya with the title 'Rashtrapati', See *SWJN*, Vol. 8, 1st Series, pp. 520–23.

14 Speech at a public meeting in Calcutta, 1 January 1952. A.I.R. tapes, N.M.M.L. (Original in Hindi), *SWJN*, 2nd Series, Vol. 17, pp. 73–80

15 Quoted in Purushottam Agrawal, *Who is Bharat Mata, On History, Culture and Idea of India: Writings by and on Jawaharlal Nehru*, (New Delhi: Speaking Tiger, 2019), pp. 468-70. Emphasis mine.

16 C.D. Deshmukh, *The Course of My Life*, (Delhi: Orient Longman, 1974), p. 205.

17 *SWJN*, 2nd Series, Vol. 4, p. 208.

18 See Rakesh Batabyal, *JNU: The Making of a University*, (Delhi: Harper Collins, 2014).

19 *The New Indian Express*, 23 July 2024 https://www.newindianexpress.com/cities/delhi/2020/Jan/10/cab-auto-rickshaw-drivers-refusing-to-go-to-jnu-post-violence-2087716.html and The Wire, 26 March 2024, https://thewire.in/rights/jnu-

elections-students-body-left-right both accessed on
23 July 2024.

Economic Development with Democracy and Sovereignty

1   See e.g., Minutes of the fourth meeting of the
    National Development Council, New Delhi, 6 May
    1955, File No 17 (17&/56-PMS) in *SWJN,* 2nd
    Series, Vol. 28, p. 371. See also my 'Introduction' in
    Aditya Mukherjee, ed., *A Centenary History of the
    Indian National Congress,* Vol. V, 1964–84, (New
    Delhi: Academic Publishers, 2011). Emphasis mine.

2   See Aditya Mukherjee, 'Empire: How Colonial
    India made Modern Britain', *Economic and Political
    Weekly,* Vol. XLV, No. 50, 11 December 2010 and
    Ch. 2 in *Political Economy of Colonial and Post-
    Colonial India,* for a detailed discussion on how
    colonial surplus appropriation aided the process of
    primitive accumulation in the West.

3   4 June 1949, *LCM,* Vol. 1, 1985, p. 371.

4   A. Vaidyanathan, 'The Indian Economy Since
    Independence (1947–70)', in Dharma Kumar, ed.,
    The Cambridge Economic History of India, Vol. II,

(Orient Blackswan, Delhi, 2005), p. 961. Emphasis mine.

5   See Aditya Mukherjee, 'Planned Development in India 1947–65: The Nehruvian Legacy', in Shigeru Akita, ed., *South Asia in the 20th Century International Relations,* Tokyo, 2000. Also in Bipan Chandra, Mridula Mukherjee, Aditya Mukherjee, *India Since Independence,* Ch. 25. These figures are from an extremely persuasive piece by Vijay Kelkar, 'India and the World Economy: A Search for Self-Reliance', Paper read at seminar on Jawaharlal Nehru and Planned Development, New Delhi, 1980, reprinted in *Economic and Political Weekly,* Vol. 15, No. 5/7, February 1980.

6   See Aditya Mukherjee, 'Planning and the Public Sector: Perspectives of the Capitalists and the Nehruvian Left', in *Political Economy of Colonial and Post-Colonial India.* See also, Aditya Mukherjee, *Imperialism, Nationalism and the Making of the Indian Capitalist Class,* (New Delhi: Sage, 2002), Chapters 10 and 11.

7   Pulapre Balakrishnan, 'The Recovery of India: Economic Growth in the Nehru Era', *Economic and*

Political Weekly, Vol. 42, Nos. 45–46, 17 November 2007, Table 4, pp. 62–63.

8   Ibid.

9   These figures are from Vijay Kelkar, 'India and the World Economy.'

10 See, for example, Tirthankar Roy, 'Economic Legacies of Colonial Rule in India: Another Look', *Economic and Political Weekly,* Vol. 50, No. 15, 11 April 2015.

11 Address at Bhoothalingam Centenary celebrations, Nehru Memorial Museum and Library, New Delhi, 21 February 2009, organized by the National Council of Applied Economic Research. See also his *Rediscovery of India* (London: Bloomsbury, 2011).

12 See Aditya Mukherjee, 'Return of the Colonial in Indian Economic History: The Last Phase of Colonialism in India,' Presidential Address, 68th session of the Indian History Congress (Modern India), 2007, in Aditya Mukherjee, *Political Economy of Colonial and Post-Colonial India,* and for a very similar understanding see the insightful article by Pulapre Balakrishnan, 'The Recovery of India: Economic Growth in the Nehru Era, *EPW,* Vol. 42, No. 45–46, 17 November 2007.

13 K.N. Raj, *Indian Economic Growth: Performance and Prospects,* New Delhi, 1965, p. 2.

14 The figures are based on Angus Maddison, *The World Economy:* p. 643. S. Sivasubramonian and A. Heston's estimates show an annual growth rate of per capita income between 1914 and 1946, which is somewhat higher at 0.26 per cent and 0.13 per cent, respectively but nevertheless prove our point, reflecting the sharp contrast between before and after Independence. M. Mukherjee's estimates of income growth are much lower than even Maddison's. See R. W. Goldsmith, *The Financial Development of India,*1860–1977, (New Haven: Yale University Press, 1983), Table 1.2, p. 4.

15 West Europe as a whole grew at 1.88 per cent between 1973–2001. Maddison, *The World Economy*, p. 643.

16 Figures for 2001–07 are based on *Economic Survey, 2006–07,* Government of India, New Delhi, 2007, Table 1.2, S-4, and Aditya Mukherjee, 'Indian Economy in the New Millennium,' in Bipan Chandra, Mridula Mukherjee and Aditya Mukherjee, *India Since Independence.* I have taken the per capita income growth rate for 2006–07 at a conservative 8 per cent. Sivasubramonian's comprehensive and detailed

study confirms the sharp break in aggregate growth rates as well as in different sectors of the economy between 1900–47 and 1947–2000. See, e.g., S. Sivasubramonian, *The National Income of India in the Twentieth Century* (New Delhi: Oxford University Press, 2000), Table 9.35, Fig. 9.5, pp. 622–28.

17 See, for example, Irfan Habib, 'Colonization of the Indian Economy 1757–1900', in *Essays in Indian History, Towards a Marxist Perception* (New Delhi: Tulika, 1995), pp. 304–05 and Bipan Chandra, chapter on 'The Colonial Legacy' in Bipan Chandra, Mridula Mukherjee, Aditya Mukherjee, *India Since Independence,* p.12.

18 See A.K. Bagchi, *Private Investment in India, 1900– 1939, Cambridge*, 1972, p. 160 and A.K. Bannerji, *India's Balance of Payments: Estimates of Current and Capital Accounts from 1921–22 to 1938–39* (Bombay: Asia Publishing House, 1963), pp. 195 and 200.

19 See Aditya Mukherjee, 'The Return of the Colonial Perspective in Indian Economic History: The Last Phase of Colonialism in India' in *Political Economy of Colonial and Post-Colonial India,* Ch. 1, Table 1.3, p. 68.

20 Calculated from Jagdish Bhagwati and Padma Desai, *India Planning for Industrialisation,* (London: Oxford University Press), 1970, p. 74.

21 See Aditya Mukherjee, 'Indira Gandhi: Shaping the Indian Economy, from Increased Dirigisme to Economic Reform', Ch. 16 in *Political Economy of Colonial and Post-colonial India,* and my chapter, 'Indian Economy 1965–1991', in Bipan Chandra et al., *India Since Independence,* for a discussion on the changes in the internal situation, the global situation and the nature of world capitalism, requiring a shift in economic strategy.

22 George Blyn, *Agricultural Trends in India, 1891– 1947: Output, Availability, and Productivity* (Philadelphia: University of Pennsylvania Press, 1966), p. 123 and p. 102. See also Goldsmith, *The Financial Development of India,* p. 68.

23 Jawaharlal Nehru, *Speeches,* Vol. 2, Publications Division, GOI, New Delhi, 1954, p. 89. Emphasis mine.

24 Resolution on 'The general political situation in the country and the Congress' drafted by Nehru on 6 March 1952 and adopted with minor changes, at the meeting of the All India Congress Committee in

Calcutta on 22 March 1952, *SWJN,* 2nd Series, Vol. 17, p. 142. Emphasis mine.

25 See my chapters 29–32 in *India Since Independence* ...

26 Jagdish Bhagwati and Padma Desai, *Planning for Industrialisation,* p. 74 and Table 25.3, Growth in Infrastructure Health and Education, in 'Indian Economy, 1947–1965: The Nehruvian Legacy', in *India Since Independence,* p. 454.

27 See George Blyn, *Agricultural Trends in India, 1891–1947: Output, Availability, and Productivity,* Table 5.8, p. 119, K.N. Raj, *Indian Economic Growth: Performance and Prospects,* (Delhi: Allied Publishers, 1965), for the pre- and post-Independence figures, respectively. See also Mridula Mukherjee, *Colonialising Agriculture: The Myth of Punjab Exceptionalism* (New Delhi: Sage, 2006). See also my chapters 29–33, discussing the Land reforms and the Green Revolution, in *India Since Independence.*

28 G.S. Bhalla, 'Nehru and Planning—Choices in Agriculture,' *Working Paper Series,* School of Social Sciences, Jawaharlal Nehru University, New Delhi, 1990, p. 29. Emphasis mine.

29 See, for a detailed discussion, my chapters (29–33) on Land Reform and The Green Revolution in Bipan Chandra, Mridula Mukherjee, Aditya Mukherjee, *India Since Independence* . . .

30 Daniel Thorner, *The Shaping of Modern India* (New Delhi: Allied Publishers, 1980), p. 245. Addition in parenthesis mine.

31 See 'Indian Economy, 1947–65: The Nehruvian Legacy', in Bipan Chandra, Mridula Mukherjee and Aditya Mukherjee, *India Since Independence* . . .

32 The statistics given here are from Jagdish Bhagwati and Padma Desai, *Planning for Industrialisation*, 1970, p. 74.

Keeping the Focus on the Poor

1 Sukhamoy Chakravarty, *Development Planning: The Indian Experience*, (Delhi, Oxford University Press, 1987), p. 83

2 *LCM,* 16 June 1952, Vol. 3, p. 18.

3 Jawaharlal Nehru, *Speeches*, Vol. 2, (New Delhi: Publications Division, 1983), pp. 50–56.

4 See my chapter on Cooperatives and an Overview of Land Reforms in Bipan Chandra, Mridula

Mukherjee, Aditya Mukherjee, *India Since Independence*.

5   *LCM*, 5 July 1952, Vol. 3, pp. 38–39. Emphasis mine.

6   Hiren Mukherjee, *The Gentle Colossus: A Study of Jawaharlal Nehru*, (Calcutta: Manisha Granthalay, 1960), p.52.

7   Sardar Patel, the Home Minister, being a fine criminal lawyer, was convinced of Savarkar's guilt and told Jawaharlal Nehru in unambiguous terms, 'It was a fanatical wing of the Hindu Mahasabha directly under Savarkar that [hatched] the conspiracy and saw it through'. See, Durga Das, ed., *Sardar Patel Correspondence, 1945–50*, Vol. VI, (Ahmedabad, Navajivan Publishing House, 1971–74), p. 56. Also, a Commission of Inquiry was set up in 1966 under Justice Jeevan Lal Kapur, a former judge of the Supreme Court of India, to look into the conspiracy to assassinate Gandhiji. After three years of investigation, the Commission came to the following conclusion, 'All these facts taken together were destructive of any theory other than the conspiracy to murder by Savarkar and his group'. Jeevan Lal Kapur, *Report of Commission of Inquiry*

into Conspiracy to Murder Mahatma Gandhi, New Delhi, 1970, para 25.106. p. 303.

8   Bipan Chandra, 'Jawaharlal Nehru in Historical Perspective', in *The Writings of Bipan Chandra: The Making of Modern India from Marx to Gandhi*, for an incisive analysis of Nehru, particularly the nature of his vision of 'socialism' and social transformation.

9   *Ibid.*, chapters 1 and 2.

10 Jawaharlal Nehru, *Speeches*, Vol. 2, p. 392, quoted in Bipan Chandra, 'Jawaharlal Nehru in Historical Perspective'.

11 *Discovery*, p. 441. Emphasis mine.

12 https://www.globalhungerindex.org/pdf/en/2023/India.pdf and https://www.globalhungerindex.org/ranking.html accessed on 23 November 2023.

Scientific Temper

1   *Discovery,* pp. 570–71.

2   *The Guardian,* 28 October 2014, https://www.theguardian.com/world/2014/oct/28/indian-prime-minister-genetic-science-existed-ancient-times accessed on 19 August 2021.

3 *Hindustan Times,* 14 January 2020, https://www.hindustantimes.com/india-news/arjunas-s-arrows-had-nuclear-power-chariots-flew-says-bengal-governor-dhankhar-draws-flak/story-M185xVdjIP8JbzTsSDRkOJ.html accessed on 19 August 2021.

4 See the RSS mouthpiece, *Organiser,* 4 November 2001.

5 See, for example, https://www.bbc.com/news/av/world-asia-india-51997699, BBC, 22 March 2020, accessed on 25 July 2024, *Business Standard,* 4 April 2020, https://www.business-standard.com/article/pti-stories/shining-torches-in-sky-won-t-solve-problem-rahul-gandhi-on-covid-19-1200404 00791_1.html, accessed on 25 July, *The Economic Times,* 2 March 2020, https://economictimes.indiatimes.com/news/politics-and-nation/gaum utra-gobar-may-cure-coronavirus-bjp-mla-tells-assam-assembly/articleshow/74444488.cms? from=mdr, accessed on 26 July 2024.

6 *The Hindu,* 9 July 2024, https://www.thehindu.com/news/national/stopped-sale-of-14-products-whose-manufacturing-licences-were-suspended-

patanjali-to-supreme-court/article68384183.ece accessed on 24 July 2024 and BBC, 18 April 2024, https://www.bbc.com/news/world-asia-india-6881 6285 accessed on 24 July 2024.

Bibliography

Anderson, Perry, *The Indian Ideology*, Three Essays Collective, Gurgaon, 2012.

Apoorvanand, 'Why JNU's Ethos Continues to be Politically Relevant in India', *The Wire*, 26 March 2024, https://thewire.in/rights/jnu-elections-students-body-left-right

Azad, Rohit, et.al., ed., *What the Nation Really Needs to Know: The JNU Nationalism Lectures*, Harper Collins, Noida, 2016.

Bagchi, A.K., *Private Investment in India, 1900-1939*, Cambridge University Press, *Cambridge*, 1972.

Balakrishnan, Pulapre, 'The Recovery of India: Economic Growth in the Nehru Era', *Economic and Political Weekly*, Vol. XLII, Nos. 45-46, 17 November 2007.

Balakrishnan, Pulapre, *India's Economy from Nehru to Modi: A Brief History*, Permanent Black and Ashoka University, Ranikhet, 2022.

Bannerji, A.K., *India's Balance of Payments: Estimates of Current and Capital Accounts from 1921-22 to1938-39*, Asia Publishing House, Bombay, 1963.

Batabyal, Rakesh, *Communalism in Bengal: From Famine to Noakhali*, Sage, New Delhi, 2005.

Batabyal, Rakesh, *JNU: The Making of a University*, Harper Collins, Delhi, 2014.

Bhagwati, Jagdish and Padma Desai, *India Planning for Industrialisation: Industrialization and Trade Policies Since 1951*, Oxford University Press, London, 1970.

Bhalla, G. S., 'Nehru and Planning – Choices in Agriculture', *Working Paper Series*, School of Social Sciences, Jawaharlal Nehru University, New Delhi, 1990.

Bhattacharjee, Manash Firaq, *Nehru and the Spirit of India*, Viking, Gurugram, 2022.

Bhattacharya, A.K., and Paranjoy Guha Thakurta, 'Contours of Crony Capitalism in the Modi Raj', in Angana P. Chatterji, Thomas Blom Hansen and Christophe Jaffrelot, eds., *Majoritarian State: How*

Hindu Nationalism is Changing India, Oxford University Press, 2019.

Biswas, Soutik, "Invisible in our own country': Being Muslim in Modi's India'. https://www.bbc.com/news/world-asia-india-68498675

Blyn, George, *Agricultural Trends in India, 1891–1947: Output, Availability, and Productivity*, University of Pennsylvania Press, Philadelphia, 1966.

Brecher, Michael, *Nehru: A Political Biography*, Oxford University Press, London, 1959.

Burbank, Jane, Keynote Lecture on 'Empire and Transformation: The Politics of Difference' at the 6th International Symposium of Comparative Research on Major Regional Powers in Eurasia Comparing Modern Empires: Imperial Rule and Decolonisation in the Changing World Order, Hokkaido University, Japan, 20 January 2012.

Burbank, Jane and Frederick Cooper, *Empire in World History: Power and Politics of Difference*, Princeton University Press, New Jersey 2010.

Camille, Auvray, 'Crony capitalism in Modi's India', Le Monde diplomatique – English, https://mondediplo.com/2024/04/04india. 19 Apr 2024.

Casolari, Marzia, 'Hindutva's Foreign Tie Up in the 1930s: Archival Evidence', *EPW*, 22 January 2000: 218–228.

Casolari, Marzia, *In the Shadow of the Swastika: Relationships between Indian Radical Nationalism, Italian Fascism and Nazism*, Routledge, Oxon and New York, 2020.

Chakravarty, Sukhamoy, *Development Planning: The Indian Experience*, Oxford University Press, Delhi, 1987.

Chandra, Bipan, *Communalism in Modern India*, Vikas, New Delhi, 1984 (Har-Anand, New Delhi, 3rd revised edition, 2008).

Chandra, Bipan, 'Jawaharlal Nehru in Historical Perspective', in *Writings of Bipan Chandra: The Making of Modern India: From Marx to Gandhi*, Orient Blackswan, 2012.

Chandra, Bipan, *Writings of Bipan Chandra: The Making of Modern India: From Marx to Gandhi*, Orient Blackswan, New Delhi, 2012.

Chandra, Bipan, Mridula Mukherjee, Aditya Mukherjee, K.N. Panikkar and Sucheta Mahajan. *India's Struggle for Independence, 1857–1947*. Penguin, New Delhi, 1988.

Chandra, Bipan, Mridula Mukherjee, Aditya Mukherjee, *India Since Independence*, Penguin, New Delhi, 2008.

Dalrymple, William, 'India: The War Over History', *The New York Review of Books*, Vol. 52, No. 6, April 2005.

Desai, Meghnad, *Rediscovery of India*, Bloomsbury, London, 2011.

Deshmukh, C.D., *The Course of my Life*, Orient Longman, Delhi, 1974.

Durga Das, ed., *Sardar Patel Correspondence, 1945–50*, Vol. VI, Navajivan Publishing House, Ahmedabad, 1971–74.

Dutt, V. P., *India's Foreign Policy*, Vikas, New Delhi, 1984.

Fernée, Tadd Graham, 'The Gandhian Circle of Moral Consideration', *Social Scientist*, Vol. 50, Nos 11–12, November–December 2022.

Fernée, Tadd Graham, *Enlightenment and Violence: Modernity and Nation Making*, Sage Series in Modern Indian History, Sage, New Delhi, 2014.

Fernée, Tadd Graham, *Beyond the Circle of Violence and Progress: Ethics and Material Development in India and Egypt, Anti-colonial Struggle to Independence*, Indian Institute of Advanced Study, Shimla, 2023.

Gandhi, Mahatma, *Collected Works of Mahatma Gandhi*, Publications Division, Government of India, New Delhi, 1958–84, Various volumes.

Goldsmith, R. W., *The Financial Development of India, 1860–1977*, Yale University Press, New Haven, 1983.

Gopal, S., *Jawaharlal Nehru: A Biography*, Oxford University Press, New Delhi, Vol. 1 1975, Vol. II 1979, Vol. III 1984.

Gupta, N. L., ed., *Nehru on Communalism*, Sampradayikta Virodhi Committee, New Delhi, 1965.

Habib, Irfan, 'Colonization of the Indian Economy, 1757–1900', in *Essays in Indian History, Towards a Marxist Perception*, Tulika, New Delhi, 1995.

Habib, Irfan, 'Jawaharlal Nehru's Historical Vision', in Irfan Habib, *The National Movement: Studies in Ideology and History*, Tulika Books, New Delhi, 2011.

Habib, Irfan, *The National Movement: Studies in Ideology and History*, Tulika Books, New Delhi, 2011

Habib, Irfan, Suvira Jaiswal and Aditya Mukherjee, *History in the New NCERT Textbooks: A Report and Index of Errors*, approved and published by the Executive Committee of the Indian History Congress, Kolkata, 2003.

Heidrich, Joachim, 'Jawaharlal Nehru's Perception of History', (Mimeo.), in Seminar on 'Jawaharlal Nehru as Writer and Historian', organised by the Jawaharlal Nehru Memorial Fund and Jawaharlal Nehru Memorial Museum and Library, New Delhi, 23–26 October 1989.

Jaffrelot, Christophe, *The Hindu Nationalist Movement in India,* Columbia University Press, New York, 1998.

Jaffrelot, Christophe, *Hindu Nationalism: A Reader,* Permanent Black, Ranikhet, 2009.

Jagannathan, R., 'A more nuanced democracy: There is no need for it to be only what the West says it must be' https://timesofindia.indiatimes.com/blogs/toi-edit-page/a-more-nuanced-democracy-there-is-no-need-for-it-to-be-only-what-the-west-says-it-must-be/

Kapur, Jeevan Lal, *Report of Commission of Inquiry into Conspiracy to Murder Mahatma Gandhi,* New Delhi, 1970.

Kelkar, Vijay, 'India and the World Economy: A Search for Self-Reliance', paper read at Seminar on Jawaharlal Nehru and Planned Development, New

Delhi, 1980, reprinted in *Economic and Political Weekly*, Vol. 15, No. 5/7, February 1980.

Krishna, Chaitanya, ed., *Fascism in India: Faces, Fangs and Facts*, Manak, New Delhi, 2003.

Maddison, Angus, *The World Economy: A Millennial Perspective*, vol. I, *Historical Statistics*, Vol. 2, OECD, 2006; Indian edition, New Delhi, 2007.

Mahajan, Sucheta, *Independence and Partition: The Erosion of Colonial Power in India*, Sage, New Delhi, 2000.

Mukherjee, Aditya, 'Planned Development in India, 1947-65: The Nehruvian Legacy', in Shigeru Akita, ed., *South Asia in the 20th Century International Relations*, Tokyo, 2000

Mukherjee, Aditya, *Imperialism, Nationalism and the Making of the Indian Capitalist Class: 1920–1947*, Sage, New Delhi, 2002, new edition in Penguin forthcoming.

Mukherjee, Aditya, 'Empire: How Colonial India made Modern Britain', *Economic and Political Weekly*, Vol. 45, No. 50, 11 December 2010.

Mukherjee, Aditya, ed., *A Centenary History of the Indian National Congress*, Vol. V, 1964–84, New Delhi, 2011.

Mukherjee, Aditya, 'Inclusive Democracy and People's Empowerment: The Legacy of Jawaharlal Nehru', *EPW*, Vol. 50, No. 16, 18 April 2015.

Mukherjee, Aditya, 'Return of the Colonial in Indian Economic History: The Last Phase of Colonialism in India', Presidential Address, 68th session of the Indian History Congress (Modern India), 2007, reproduced as Chapter 1 in Aditya Mukherjee, *Political Economy of Colonial and Post-Colonial India*, Primus Books, Delhi, 2022.

Mukherjee, Aditya, 'Colonialism and Communalism: A Legacy Haunting India Today', in Aditya Mukherjee, *Political Economy of Colonial and Post-Colonial India*, Primus Books, Delhi, 2022.

Mukherjee, Aditya, *Political Economy of Colonial and Post-Colonial India*, Primus Books, Delhi, 2022.

Mukherjee, Aditya, 'A Relook at Jawaharlal Nehru', *The Wire*, 17 June 2023, https://m.thewire.in/article/books/a-relook-at-jawaharlal-nehru

Mukherjee, Aditya, Mridula Mukherjee and Sucheta Mahajan, *RSS, School Texts and the Murder of Mahatma Gandhi: The Hindu Communal Project*, Sage, New Delhi, 2008, an enlarged revised edition forthcoming shortly with Penguin.

Mukherjee, Aditya and Mridula Mukherjee, 'Weaponising History: The Hindutva Communal Project' *The Wire,* 10 April 2023, https://m.thewire.in/article/history/weaponising-history-the-hindu-communal-project;

Mukherjee, Mridula, *Colonialising Agriculture: The Myth of Punjab Exceptionalism*, Sage Publications, New Delhi, 2006.

Mukherjee, Mridula, 'History Wars: The Case of Gandhi-Nehru-Patel', in IIC Quarterly, Vol. 49, No. 1, Summer 2022.

Mukherjee, Mridula, "Foreign Policy: The Nehru Era", in Bipan Chandra, Mridula Mukherjee and Aditya Mukherjee, *India Since Independence,* Penguin, New Delhi, 2008.

Mukherjee, Mridula, "Jawaharlal Nehru's Finest Hour: The Struggle for a Secular India", *Studies in People's History,* Vol. 1, No. 2, 2014, https://journals.sagepub.com/doi/abs/10.1177/2348448914549900?journalCode=sipa

Mukherjee, Mridula, 'Communal Threat and Secular Resistance: From Noakhali to Gujarat', *Presidential Address (Modern India), Indian History Congress,* 2011.

Mukherjee, Mridula, 'Civil Liberties and Indian Nationalism', in Rohit Azad et.al., ed., *What the Nation Really Needs to Know: The JNU Nationalism Lectures*, Harper Collins, Noida, 2016.

Mukherjee, Mridula and Aditya Mukherjee, *Communalisation of Education: The History Textbooks Controversy*, with an introduction by the authors, Delhi Historians' Group, Delhi, 2002.

Mukherjee, Pranab, Aditya Mukherjee, et.al., eds., *Congress and the Making of the Indian Nation*, Vol. II, Academic Publishers, New Delhi, 2011.

Nanda, B.R., ed., *Indian Foreign Policy: The Nehru Years*, Vikas, Delhi, 1976.

Naqvi, Saba, '2024 General Election is a Masterclass in Crony Capitalism and Authoritarianism', Frontline, 30 March 2024, https://frontline.thehindu.com/columns/2024-general-election-crony-capitalism-authoritarianism-ed-raids-and-arrests/article68006060.ece

Nehru, Jawaharlal, *Jawaharlal Nehru's Speeches*, Vol. 1 (1946–49), Publications Division, Government of India, New Delhi, 4th edition 1983.

Nehru, Jawaharlal, *Jawaharlal Nehru's Speeches,* Vol. 4, 1957–63, Publications Division, Government of India, New Delhi, 1964

Nehru, Jawaharlal, *An Autobiography*, (first published 1936 by John Lane, The Bodley Head Ltd., London), Jawaharlal Nehru Memorial Fund and Oxford University Press, New Delhi, 1980.

Nehru, Jawaharlal, *Recent Writings and Essays*, Kitabistan, Allahabad, 1937.

Nehru, Jawaharlal, *Glimpses of World History*, (first published in two volumes, 1934–35, by Kitabistan, Allahabad,), Jawaharlal Nehru Memorial Fund and Oxford University Press, 1982.

Nehru, Jawaharlal, *Discovery of India* (first published by The Signet Press, Calcutta 1946), Penguin, Gurgaon, 2010.

Nehru, Jawaharlal, *Selected Works of Jawaharlal Nehru, (SWJN)*, 1st Series and 2nd Series, New Delhi, Various volumes.

Nehru, Jawaharlal, *Jawaharlal Nehru: Letters to Chief Ministers* (*LCM*), New Delhi, 1985, Vols. 1–5.

Patnaik, Prabhat, 'Fascism Arrives in Camouflage', *The Telegraph Online*, 15 August 2022, http://www.telegraphindia.com/india/fascism-arrives-in-camouflage-says-prabhat-patnaik/cid/1880205

Patnaik, Prabhat, 'The Fascism of our Times', *Social Scientist*, Vol. 21, Nos. 3/4, March–April 1993.

Raj, K N., *Indian Economic Growth: Performance and Prospects,* New Delhi, 1965

Robinson, Francis, *Separatism Among Indian Muslims: The Politics of the United Provinces' Muslims, 1860–1923*, Cambridge University Press, Cambridge, 1974.

Roy, Arundhati, 'The Dismantling of Democracy in India will Affect the Whole World', *Scroll.in*, 14 September 2023, https://scroll.in/article/1055943/arundhati-roy-the-dismantling-of-democracy-in-india-will-affect-the-whole-world.

Roy, Tirthankar, 'Economic Legacies of Colonial Rule in India: Another Look', *Economic and Political Weekly (EPW)*, Vol. 50, No. 15, 11 April 2015.

Sen, Amartya, 'The Threats to Secular India', *The New York Review,* 8 April 1993.

Sen, Amartya, *The Idea of Justice,* Allen Lane, London, 2009.

Sen, Amartya, *The Argumentative Indian: Writings on Indian History, Culture and Identity,* Penguin, London, 2005.

Sen, Amartya, 'History and the Enterprise of Knowledge', Address delivered at the Indian History Congress, Calcutta, January 2001.

Sivasubramonian, S., *The National Income of India in the Twentieth Century*, Oxford University Press, New Delhi, 2000.

Smith, W.C., *Modern Islam in India: A Social Analysis*, Victor Gollancz, London 1946.

Srinivasan, R., The Wire, 3 May 2024, https://thewire.in/media/how-indian-corporate-giants-have-been-tightening-their-grip-over-the-media

Stanley, Jason, *How Fascism Works: The Politics of Us and Them*, Random House, New York, 2018.

Stanley, Jason, 'The US should not normalize Modi's autocratic and Illiberal India at the G20', *Guardian*, 8 September 2023, https://www.theguardian.com/commentisfree/2023/sep/08/biden-india-modi-g20-autocrat

Thapar, Romila, 'Perspectives of the History of Somanatha', Umashankar Joshi Memorial Lecture, 29 December 2012.

Thapar, Romila, *Somanatha: The Many Voices of a History*, Penguin, New Delhi, 2003.

Thapar, Romila, Harbans Mukhia and Bipan Chandra, *Communalism and the Writing of Indian History*, People's Publishing House, Delhi, 1969.

Thorner, Daniel, *The Shaping of Modern India*, Allied, New Delhi, 1980.

Torri, Michelguglielmo, 'For a New Periodization of Indian History: The History of India as Part of the History of the World', *Studies in History*, Vol. 30, Issue 1, 12 May 2014.

Torri, Michelguglielmo, 'India 2020: The Deepening Crisis of Democracy', *Asia Maior*, Vol. 31, 2020.

Vaidyanathan, A., 'The Indian Economy Since Independence (1947–70)', in Dharma Kumar, ed., *The Cambridge Economic History of India*, Vol. II, (First published Cambridge University Press, 1983) Orient Blackswan, Delhi, 2005.

Varshney, Ashutosh, 'Gujarat 2002 was independent India's first full-blooded pogrom. Delhi 1984 was a semi-pogrom', ThePrint, 26 February 2020, https://theprint.in/opinion/gujarat-2002-was-independent-indias-first-full-blooded-pogrom-delhi-1984-was-a-semi-pogrom/371684

Index

Scan QR code to access the
Penguin Random House India website

Parkash. 120072
17-12-24 mL